T0167268

FREEMASONRY
THREADED
THROUGH
MORMONISM

FREEMASONRY THREADED THROUGH MORMONISM

Jay M. Hawkinson

FREEMASONRY THREADED THROUGH MORMONISM

Copyright © 2014 Jay M. Hawkinson.

All rights reserved. No part of this book may be used or reproduced by any means, graphic, electronic, or mechanical, including photocopying, recording, taping or by any information storage retrieval system without the written permission of the author except in the case of brief quotations embodied in critical articles and reviews.

iUniverse books may be ordered through booksellers or by contacting:

iUniverse
1663 Liberty Drive
Bloomington, IN 47403
www.iuniverse.com
1-800-Authors (1-800-288-4677)

Because of the dynamic nature of the Internet, any web addresses or links contained in this book may have changed since publication and may no longer be valid. The views expressed in this work are solely those of the author and do not necessarily reflect the views of the publisher, and the publisher hereby disclaims any responsibility for them.

Any people depicted in stock imagery provided by Thinkstock are models, and such images are being used for illustrative purposes only. Certain stock imagery © Thinkstock.

ISBN: 978-1-4917-2040-0 (sc)
ISBN: 978-1-4917-2041-7 (e)

Library of Congress Control Number: 2014903345

Print information available on the last page.

iUniverse rev. date: 06/26/2018

CONTENTS

About the author: The author grew up in the Western Illinois Area known as Quad Cities U.S.A. The Quad Cities[1] is located along the Mississippi River and it comprises five cities: Milan, Rock Island, East Moline, Moline, and Silvis on the Illinois side and two cities: Davenport and Bettendorf on the Iowa side of the river. Except for a five year tour in the U.S. Air Force and five years living and working in Rockford, Illinois, he remained in the Quad Cities area until 2010 when he relocated in Rapid City, South Dakota. Academically, he attended Black Hawk College in Moline and Augustana College in Rock Island, as well as completing a variety of courses with various other colleges and technical schools.

He has traveled to every state in the U.S. except Alaska, traveled in Europe and spent one year working in British Columbia. Of his many business activities, he owned his own small manufacturing business for over ten years during which time he received two U.S. Patents for a water recycling system.

His Masonic career began in 1950 when he was initiated into the Chalmers J. Seymour Chapter, Order of DeMolay in Moline. DeMolay was, and remains, a Masonic youth organization for young men. While growing up with DeMolay, he became the Chapter Master Councilor, or leader, and remained active in the Illinois State wide DeMolay organization. As a result of his DeMolay contributions, he was awarded the Chevalier distinction and the Legion of Honor. He was later awarded

---

[1] The Quad Cities was originally known as the Tri-Cities for many years denoting the cities: Rock Island, Moline and Davenport. As the area grew and cities were added, the popular name never exceeded the Quad Cities. Quint Cities was tried but it did not last. Moline is where John Deere put down his roots and formed the world wide business that carries his name today. The John Deere Headquarters remains in Moline.

the Advisor Cross of Honor for his 14 plus years serving as the chapter's Masonic advisor.

At the age of 21, the author became a Master Mason in Moline Lodge #1014. In 1968 he became a 32° Scottish Rite Mason in the Illinois Valley of Moline. He remained very active in Masonry and served as a leader for many Masonic projects. He edited and published the Scottish Rite newsletter which received a Franklin Honorable Mention award from the Northern Masonic Jurisdiction of the Scottish Rite. Officially, through his Masonic career, he served as leader of the Lodge of Perfection for four years, functioned as Valley Secretary for two years, and served as Commander-in-Chief of the Scottish Rite Consistory for two years. He was awarded the Illinois Distinguished Service Award in 1982 and in 1986 was coroneted as an Honorary 33rd Degree Scottish Rite Mason for the Northern Masonic Jurisdiction. In year 2007 he achieved a 50 year member status in Freemasonry.

The author takes pleasure in researching Masonic history and writing articles to publish and share. He has written and shared articles about the Cherokee Masons in the "Trail of Tears" and. Another article relates the less known but outstanding Masonic accomplishments made by General Douglas MacArthur.

PREFACE

Historically, the Masonic Order is believed to have begun during the construction of King Solomon's Temple. King Solomon's temple was built and dedicated to the Lord God Jehovah in the year of the world 2992, or 1012 full years before the Christian era. The temple was constructed near Jerusalem on Mt Moriah. In preparation for the actual temple construction, a neighboring King and ally, Hiram King of Tyre, willingly gathered his best artisans and sent them as an army of skilled craftsmen to build Solomon's temple in Jerusalem. Among the army of craftsmen was a highly skilled work superintendent named: Hiram Abif (Abif meaning master or chief operator) to oversee all temple construction. Hiram, King of Tyre also was the suppler for timbers that were delivered from Lebanon forests and used in the construction. The rank and file of assembled builders was grouped into three artisan skill levels: helpers were known as starting apprentices, then those with advanced skills were known as fellows and those highly experienced were respected masters of their trade. Regardless of their individual skill levels, all craftsmen maintained a rigid respect for the men of each skill level, and each man normally aspired to advance to a higher skill level as an opportunity was presented. The band-of-artisans or craftsmen were collectively proud of their work but they were also jealous and extremely wary of any and all intruders, so they guarded their work with their lives. All temple craftsmen met together once daily to pray, discuss their achievements and learn new work that yet needed to be done in the temple construction. Hiram Abif remained ever watchful over the quality of all work and he only accepted the finest work. He faithfully attended to this duty by carefully inspecting all work-in-progress at noon each day.

When Solomon's Temple was completed and dedicated, the close knit brotherhood of craftsmen continued through countless generations of temple and cathedral building throughout Europe. Teams of working craftsmen often chose to maintain a special unity by organizing guilds to stay together and maintain a work bond. Over time, the worker guilds became progressively structured, guarded and secret during succeeding generations. All guild members progressively became further refined in dedicating moral support to their brother craftsmen, they developed greater strength in individual character, and assisted with a brother's family when a brother's family was in need. Then In 1717 came a "Masonic Awakening" in England. It was then that Masonry formally transitioned from being specifically connected with various craftsmen guilds and became totally adapted in developing the individual character in selected men as had been done among the craftsman. This new attitude then became available to all respectable adult men and evolved into Freemasonry as we know it today. Most important, Freemasonry included religious practices taken from its early beginning but it was never established as a religion except that to be a member demanded that the candidate and member personally believe in only one supreme-being. The supreme-being was best known by each man as the *Grand Architect of the Universe*—identified as either: Jehovah, Allah, Buda, Krishna, etc. In addition, each member was obligated to attend his *own* church and to honor his *own* personal religious beliefs according to his god. Freemasonry thereafter remained a secret order among men. It became known as a World Wide Brotherhood of Masons with each member pledging to work and aid his brother and protect all Masonic secrets with his life. By his sworn pledge each Freemason would be subject to penalties of death should the Order's secrets be revealed to any person or persons outside of the order.

The Mormon religion emerged in 1830 as a fresh new religion and it too became a secret covenant among its membership. People from all walks of life were drawn to this new religion. They became dedicated to their work for God and to aid their fellow man. As Mormonism developed, church ritualistic secrets were securely borne by each faithful member once they had been consecrated by the Church Endowment. Each endowed member vowed not to reveal any of the endowment secrets to anyone under strict life threatening penalties unless that person was an associate Latter-day Saint. Each Mormon temple was closed to the public and only the endowed Mormon was allowed entry onto the Mormon Church sanctity.

Now, to advance into the Twentieth Century . . . . When the author was ten years old, his father drove the family to Nauvoo, Illinois on Labor Day where the author was first introduced to Mormon history. That weekend happened to be the annual Nauvoo wine and cheese festival. Nauvoo was the home of a "blue cheese" plant, as well as home to a few local wine makers. On this weekend they all sold their wares and grapes at roadside stands. In the city park, long trellis fences containing concord grapes that were grown and offered free to all for the picking. Nauvoo presented a curious historical attraction because Latter-day Saint's home foundation remnants were evident throughout the city and there was an interesting small memorial park located on the city bluff that identified where the Mormon temple had once stood. The homes of Joseph Smith and Brigham Young still stood erect and were well maintained. Visitors could walk around the perimeter fences and view both homes. In other locations, large signs had been erected that announced a special "Wedding of the Wine and Cheese." This was an evening drama that was later learned to have been based on early Latter Day Saints history. The author unfortunately never was able to attend any performance.

In 1961, the author served in the United States Air Force at a SAC (Strategic Air Command) Radar Bomb Scoring Detachment in Warrington, Oregon. When off duty he met a young Latter-day Saint lady who helped him better understand the Latter-day Saints religion and philosophies. Not long after their meeting, his detachment packed up and moved to Boise, Idaho. In Boise he found that he had moved nearer to the heart of a larger population of LDS (Latter-day Saints) families. This Boise relocation provided the author a means to develop a greater understanding for the LDS.

The author returned to Illinois after his discharge from the Air Force and married a young lady he had met in Boise, Idaho. He and his new wife resumed the Labor Day trips to Nauvoo. While the author had been away, he found that much of Nauvoo had been restored. They found that many

Latter-day Saint homes and businesses once occupied by Mormons during the 1840's had been totally restored. He also found that present day Latter-day Saint church members were temporarily living in Nauvoo during the summer and were contributing their missionary time by serving as historical guides at the various restored properties. All guides were attired in 1840 period clothing and each guide explained Mormon history regarding the restored homes and businesses. Several annual visits turned out to be highly educational and imparted interesting background about the Mormon heritage.[2] Historically, the original Mormon temple had been set on fire by local anti-Mormons in the late 1840's Mormon War. Remnants were later ravaged by a tornado and finally, the remains were demolished to protect city inhabitants. Decades later, one of the Nauvoo reconstruction projects resulted in constructing a new and wonderful replacement of the magnificent original Mormon Temple. This Temple was dedicated in 2002.

Prior to enlisting in U.S. Air Force, the author had become a Freemason. He immediately found the work in Freemasonry impressive. He was fortunate to visit many Masonic lodges during his travels with the Air Force. Then he began to consider what he had learned about the Latter-day Saints and their Masonic connection. Their history and their religious beliefs began to challenge his interest. He researched more of the 1840's Mormon occupancy in Nauvoo by talking with western Illinois descendents who lived near Nauvoo. However, during further historical research on the Mormons, he learned that Joseph Smith Jr. had a special interest and involvement with the "core of Masonry." In fact, it

---

[2]   The author's wife of 17 years died unexpectedly in 1981. He then married a wonderful lady in 1983. She had lived and grew up only 28 miles from Nauvoo. They pooled their knowledge of Nauvoo Mormons and continued visits to this Illinois city.

appeared that Joseph Smith, Jr. had nearly duplicated the Masonic ritual and used it in organizing his newly created Mormon Church in 1829. When this first came to light, it immediately alarmed the author just as it had alarmed many Masons throughout history. Masons first realized in the early 1800's that their secretly protected ritual and oaths had been exposed through Mormonism and used by other than Masons. Each Mason "went-up-in-arms" because each felt a dedicated and trusting ownership of the Masonic ritual. Each Mason had subjected themselves to their oaths and obligations of secrecy, committed the essence of all ritual oaths to memory and each swore to maintain all Masonic secrets under the rigid penalties to which they had pledged themselves to.

Historical research was traced back to 1826 and the "Morgan Affair." This affair involved Captain William Morgan who made an uncompromising full public release of the Masonic secret ritual in Batavia, New York. The Captain essentially "let the cat out of bag" in 1826 when he published his "Illustration of Masonry" and made it available on the open book market for all of the public to freely read and absorb. A large part of the American population at that time thought it would surely expose and create the end of Freemasonry. This, in fact, did compromise and halted Masonry for two long decades in U.S. history. The original Morgan text: "Illustration of Masonry," can still be purchased today or viewed on the internet.

Young Joseph Smith, Jr. kept an ear to the news about the peculiar "Morgan Affair" that was being exposed in Batavia, New York, a town located not too distant from Joseph's home. The living drama happened at a time when young Joseph's inquisitive mind was mentally devising his religious ideas. By general observation at that time, Masonry appeared to go into an abrupt state of collapse. Perhaps Joseph was "at the right place at the right time" to learn what he needed to know to seed his creative ideas. He was a very talented and an adept person by apparently selecting the high moral discipline presented in Freemasonry to create a structure for his anticipated religion. Masons should actually rejoice that Joseph Smith, Jr. selected their noble source to develop a highly respected religious structure. However, at that time Masons did not appreciate or endorse Joseph Smith, Jr. for compromising and converting Masonic work from their fraternity's secret ritual.

The following historical presentation is not meant to undermine all good intent for the Mormon and the Latter-day Saints Religion or undermine the stature of Freemasonry. The established Mormon religious following is respected throughout the United States and beyond and is to be respected for its discipline, values and deep beliefs. At the same time, Masonry remains a strong fraternity to all of its World Wide Masonic members. Let us see how histories of these two foundations unfold by following the thread: "The *Thread of Masonry through Mormonism.*"

THE "THREAD" BEGINS HERE!

When gas rationing ended after World War II, the author's parents traded their mechanically deficient 1934 Chevrolet for a newer and better 1939 Chevrolet. This dependable car provided new freedom to resume short trips throughout the Midwest from their Moline, Illinois, home. Road trips were great at that time because gasoline was only 17¢ a gallon. One Labor Day they took a memorable trip to visit the annual Nauvoo Wine and Grape Heritage Festival. Nauvoo was a river town located 80 miles south of Moline and on the Illinois side of the Mississippi River 23 miles north of the borders intersecting Missouri, Iowa and Illinois. Nauvoo caught the family's interest when they learned that the town had been the seat for the Mormon Religious Colony in 1840. This trip became the first of many interesting trips to Nauvoo. Later trips especially sparked interest after the author became a Master Mason and began to find interesting correlations between Masons and Mormons. What he learned during his many observations and research follows . . . .

HOLD ON ... STEP BACK TO EARLY 1800

Joseph Smith, Jr. was in his late teens when he founded and created the Mormon religion in the year 1829. Joseph was living at that time in the Palmyra, New York area. Nauvoo, Illinois came into prominence later as the new religion grew and expanded as a church colony. Coincidently, as the Mormon Religion was created, Freemasonry was emerging from a Masonic revival (or new beginning) in England. This coincidence had an important bearing in the development of both Freemasonry and the Mormon Religion in America. Freemasonry reached America in 1727.

Masonry is known to have been organized during the building of King Solomon's Temple in the year 1012 BC. Masonry re-emerged much later in 1717 when it became recognized as Masonry is observed to this day. Prior to 1717, Masonry had functioned within groups of skilled craftsmen who had banded together to promote morality, be benevolent, and contribute to mankind by using their never changing ancient precepts. While building Solomon's Temple, the original craftsmen groups were made up of organized master craftsmen, temple builders, or craft guild members. As Masonry re-emerged in 1717, a variety of organized Masonic disciplines from various Masonic groups were merged to form one single ritual. This new ritual was accepted among primarily established English Masonic Lodges namely: Ancient York Masons, Modern Masons, Ancient Masons, and United Grand Lodge of Ancient Freemasons of England. This new modern Masonry then traveled across the ocean from England in 1727 and began it's emergence into the American British Colonies. By 1772 the American Revolution was underway and Masonic history has revealed how important Masons joined the Revolutionist to fight for American independence.

When Masonry reformed following its 1717 re-emergence, the operating ritual and structure was made standard for all Masonic Lodges as stipulated by the Grand Lodge of Ancient Freemasons of England. However, it becomes important to point out that a component of this new consolidated ritual was known as the *Royal Arch of Solomon* ritual and it had been embedded as a basic element in the Master Mason degree initiation. The *Royal Arch of Solomon* ritual had been integrated into the newly merged Master Mason degree by the "Ancient (Antient) Mason" discipline. This Masonic ritual alignment remained until 1813 at which point the *Royal Arch of Solomon* degree was removed from the fundamental three degrees as directed by the English Duke of Kent. He directed that the *Royal Arch* degree be moved into the beginning degrees of both the York Rite Masonry and the Scottish Rite Masonry. Likewise, in 1813, all segments of Masonic Craft Lodges merged to unite under The United

Grand Lodge of England. The Masonic ritual and operations became centrally the same among all organized lodges who were recognized by the Grand Lodge of England. This included all lodges in the Western Hemisphere. In effect, the Grand Lodge of England became the authority for world wide Masonry.

Our "Thread of Masonry . . ." begins with the Morgan Affair. The Morgan Affair nearly caused the total destruction of Freemasonry in America. The "Affair" centered on Captain William Morgan who was a brick mason living in Batavia, New York, from 1824 to 1826. He was actually a "person of ill repute" and uneducated, but a very shrewd operator. He frequently sought Masonic charity and seemed to survive by living "off-the-land." Masonic historians question whether he was actually a Master Mason, but he did manage to have someone vouch for him to enter Wells Lodge No. 282 in Batavia. Records show that he did receive the *Royal Arch* degree in Le Roy, New York, in 1825. Many questioned his actual full Masonic membership but somehow he did manage to participate often in Masonic work. Captain Morgan was always a ready observer and he seemed to absorb all that he witnessed as he became more attentive and involved during his lodge visits. In 1826, Captain Morgan entered into a contract with three nefarious men, one of which had not been permitted to advance in his Masonic lodge work and who therefore held a grudge against the Masons. Captain William Morgan agreed to a financial bond with his associates to receive one forth of the $500,000 in expected profits from a book he promised to compose, a book which would reveal all the secrets of Freemasonry. Streets in Batavia became alive with boasts by Captain Morgan about his writing intent. By publishing this book, he intended to expose and destroy Masonry in a hope that the Order would die.

Batavia Masons became highly disturbed when they heard rumors that Captain Morgan intended to compose a book that would expose their Masonic secrets. At any rate, the book, *"Illustrations of Masonry,"* proceeded to be published and would be ready for distribution in 1826. Not long after learning that the book would be made public, Captain Morgan was arrested for various trivial reasons and every attempt was made to disrupt his well being. After many disruptive arrests, he was ultimately jailed for a menial reason but someone came along and paid his accumulated fines. On that same September 11, 1826 day he was spirited away in a horse drawn coach manned by several men. He was taken to Ft. Niagara in Upper New York after which he disappeared. Many thought that Morgan had been killed. It was also thought that he had been instructed to escape to Canada and never again show his face in the United States. This later action was reported to have actually happened and that he was sent away with a token payment of $500 and told to stay in Canada. Regardless of his dismissal method, the *"Illustrations of Masonry"* went into print and was made available to the general public.

At the time Captain Morgan disappeared, public outcry came from all directions against the Masonic Order. Slanderous stories appeared in local newspapers proclaiming that Masons had dealt underhandedly with Captain Morgan. Freemasons totally denied having any involvement at all in the matter. Masons who knew nothing of the circumstances and story about the missing Captain William Morgan joined voluntarily in the search for his body or his possible killers. Three Masons were later apprehended and each did plead guilty to kidnap conspiracy and each fully served a term in prison. However, respective of murder, Captain Morgan's body had never been recovered. A decomposed body did wash ashore on a Niagara River bank in October 1827 just downriver from Fort Niagara. The body had no real resemblance to Captain Morgan but it was identified from its clothing as that of Timothy Monroe [or Munro] of Clark, Canada. In the months to come, the murder of missing Captain William Morgan was never proven but charges against the Masonic Order became overly exaggerated and amplified. The Masonic Order was persecuted and slandered for many long years following the incident. Known Masons and their family members were inordinately chastised by churches and society throughout a wide area of the then populated America. John Quincy Adams formed the Anti-Masonic Political Party because of growing bitterness towards all Masons. This new political party became known as the Whig Party. Masonic Lodge charters were pulled from most northeast lodges and the lodges disbanded in that part of the United States. Masons were afraid to identify themselves as being anyway connected with Freemasonry. Even family members of Masons would never admit that they ever knew any Mason. The Fraternity remained in deep disorder from 1827 to 1846. These were dark days for the craft, but to this day, Captain William Morgan's body was never found.

A NEW RELIGION BEGINS...
THE GOLDEN PLATES

Joseph Smith, Jr. was born in Sharon, Vermont, in 1805. Soon after he was born his family moved to Palmyra, New York, because farming efforts had failed for the family in Vermont. Palmyra was located in the *"burned over district"* in New York, which was so named for having absolutely no organized religion or church in the area. The *"burned over district"* had been left wide open to all types of revivalists. Charismatics seemed to dominate and hold spiritual control and influence over the people. This particular era in world history was known as the "Second Great Awakening," This era inspired religious enthusiasm towards God but also raised intense rejection for the political power and suppressive measures being made by the churches in Europe and the

American colonies. The Smith family settled into this district to live and farm. Their farm was near Manchester, New York, which was located a few miles south of Palmyra.

Young Joseph Smith, Jr. was drawn to religious studies at the age of twelve. He participated in Methodist Church classes, read the Bible, and developed an interest in Methodism. He also participated with his family in the common practice known as religious folk magic. It was quite common at that time for family members to experience visions or dreams where they felt they were vocally communicating directly with God.

Joseph Smith, Sr. and his older son, Hyrum, were generally occupied with a practice known as money digging when not farming. Joseph Jr. joined in and assisted in the money digging by using his special "seer stone." He would place the "seer stone" inside his hat, enwrap his face into the hat opening and the stone would reveal the location of treasure. Treasure digging was somewhat common in the Palmyra Area because of the numerous Indian mounds found in the surrounding hills. Metal artifacts could often be uncovered near the mounds. Joseph Jr. did admit that the digging ventures never were very profitable.

At the age of 19 Joseph was hired by the elderly Josia Stowell who asked him to come to Harmony, Pennsylvania, for the purpose of finding a hoard of buried silver. When in Harmony, he took up boarding at the Hale house while he made his treasure search attempt. Then on March 20th 1826, Joseph was arrested and brought to trial as being a "glass-looker" and a disorderly person for which he was found guilty. However, no penalty was administered for likely this was his first offense.

While boarding at the Hale house, he courted Emma Hale and soon asked for her hand in marriage. Father Hale would not approve of his request because of Joseph's meager income, which showed his inability to properly care for his daughter. Joseph and Emma then eloped and began their new life. Between 1827 and 1830 Joseph Jr. abandoned his money digging associates but he did retain his "seer stone," which he would later use in finding the buried golden religious plates.

Prior to the "Morgan Affair", Masonry, as a Brotherhood, experienced a continued membership growth in both Europe and America. Then, in 1827, the "Morgan Affair" became a drastic threat to American Masonry. The Order of Freemasons had been highly respected up to that time because their Order seemed to maintain a tried and true micro society for the men belonging to its Masonic Brotherhood. This order was in no way a religion, but to join members had to religiously believe in only one Supreme Being: "The Grand Architect of the Universe" (Also known as the one, single God worshiped by, and in the heart of each individual member). Masonry was respected for its character building and the social harmony it achieved among all of its members. The Order was also known for its success in bringing good minds together during the early formative days in America.

In Joseph Smith's family, Joseph Smith, Sr. had become a Master Mason on May 7, 1818 in Ontario Lodge No. 23 located in Canandaigu, New York. Later, his son, Hyrum Smith, became a Master Mason in Mt. Moriah Lodge No. 112 while he lived in Palmyra, New York. Both father and son had been initiated when the Royal Arch Mason degree was still embedded as an integral part of the Freemason initiation. Both father and son actively attended and participated in the Palmyra Masonic Lodge. One would expect that there was a wholesome Masonic influence and dialog at home among family members.

In 1826, highly intriguing news regarding Captain Morgan surfaced and capitalized the local news. Joseph Smith, Jr.

was drawn to the news and immersed himself in the "Morgan Affair" stories. Batavia, New York, was only a short distance away. We suspect that Joseph, in his curiosity, did acquire a copy of *"Illustrations of Masonry," written by Captain Morgan.* We expect that he did study the 184 page book and absorbed the Masonic methods and procedures presented in the book. Joseph should have also been influenced at home by Masonic dialogues between his Masonic father and brother.

Many people reading news of Timothy Monroe's dead body washing up on the Niagra River shore became a surprise because everyone thought that it would be the body of Captain William Morgan. Joseph Smith, Jr. took interest in the Morgan Affair and absorbed many details involved in that discovery. Theory is that he profoundly assimilated the name <u>Mor</u>gan to combine with <u>Mon</u>roe and created the name: "Mormon." This name assemblage combined with his on going studies of the Masonic ritual from Captain Morgan's book, became an encouraging guide to connect his religious visions with the Masonic ritual.

Back during Joseph's earlier treasure digging years he had begun experiencing divine visions whenever he was alone in isolated locations around Palmyra. Young Joseph possessed a brilliant and formative mind with which he did experience deeply moving charismatic spiritual visions. Each vision drove him more forcefully into creating a new spiritual path to his own life. In 1820, at the age of 15, he related that he had been personally visited by Jesus Christ who declared: "that all Christian denominations had become corrupt and religion had formally ended with the ultimate death of each original apostle." One evening in 1823 he was visited by an angel named Moroni who had been known as a Nephite (Ancient people thought to have left Jerusalem and settled in Central America per LDS interpretation.) during his earthly life. Moroni communicated that he had once been a prophet-warrior and revealed that before his earthly death, a set of inscribed golden plates had been sealed inside a stone box and buried in the ground near Palmyra. With the help of two angels, Urim and Thummim and his seer stone, Joseph found and later began translating directives and messages inscribed on the golden plates. The translations from the golden plates became a primary basis for his Book.

One Oliver Cowdry moved to Manchester, New York, in 1929 to serve as a school teacher. It was the custom at that time that school teachers live in the homes of students residing in the immediate school area, which he did by living with the Smith family. Oliver Cowdry was from the same area where Joseph had been born in Vermont. Like Joseph Smith, Jr., he too, had engaged in hunting for buried treasure. Oliver Cowdry arrived at an important time for Joseph Smith, Jr. It was a time when Joseph was experiencing difficulty in translating the last part of the golden plates. Oliver stepped in as a scribe to assistant in translating the whole text. When the translations were finished, Smith and Cowdry became bound as close friends and Joseph determined that they now needed to obtain a priesthood, or authority to officially act in God's name. This prophetic need, it was believed, came from that spiritual void created on earth during the *Great Apostasy*[3]. Joseph Smith, Jr. reflected back to his earlier visions where he learned that the earth

---

[3]   The Great Apostasy voiced by Joseph Smith, Jr. related to the past approximate 1633 years when the whole Christian world had been living in total spiritual darkness for lack of any acceptable religious leadership. This period spanned back to the crucifixion and death of Jesus followed by the death of His last apostle. Other Christian sects admitted that pagan gods had since become infused into all religious sects. These sects worked to attract pagans back to Christianity by amalgamating the Christian and pagan festivals such as Easter with Passover, the winter solstice with Christmas. Joseph Smith chose not to adhere to what other sects were doing.

had been left in a great religious void following the last Great Apostle's death. Joseph believed that all pastoral and spiritual guidance had been lost for a long time, as evidence of the *Apostasy*, and now religion needed to be returned to the people. In 1829, the two men went into the woods near Harmony Township in Pennsylvania where they were visited by John the Baptist who was accompanied by an angel. During this meeting the "Holy Priesthood" known as the *Priesthood of Aaron* was administered to allow permission and power to baptize. In 1831 both Joseph Smith, Jr. and Oliver Cowdry proclaimed themselves ordained in a lay ministry they called "an Apostle of Jesus Christ, an Elder of the Church" (meaning a pioneer of any great moral reform.).

Inspiration came to Joseph Smith, Jr. in 1829 (at the age of 24) as to how to build and structure the new Mormon Church. The people living in the *"burned over area"* in New York were becoming spiritually hungry for guidance in living a wholesome and religious life. By 1830 Joseph Smith had fully translated his golden plates. He sold his farm holdings to pay to publish a 584 page book: *"The Book of Mormon."* Then the idea of a Mormon Church became formally established when his book was published and distributed. The new church formation became known both as the "Church of God, or the Church of Christ." People living in the *"burned over area"* were welcomed into the new Mormon Church fold.

At the time when Joseph Smith found the golden plates on a hill top near Palmyra, he related that they had been located inside a buried sealed stone vault. The description for finding the golden plates does coincidently *"echo"* the Enoch myth presented in Royal Arch Masonry. Masonic history explains the story that during a divine vision, the Patriarch Enoch[4] was instructed to preserve the Masonic

---

4   The story of Enoch can be found in the Book of Genesis in the

mysteries for all times. Enoch was directed to carve the mysteries on golden plates (coincidently) and then place the plates in an arched stone vault within an underground temple. The temple location was marked with pillars in such a manner where King Solomon would later discover them. Masons believe that the Royal Arch ritual, as explained in the footnote, was read and absorbed by Joseph Smith, Jr. and did become incorporated as an important revelation used in developing his religion and the church endowment.

Bible. He was born in the year of the world 622 as the son of Jared and became the great-grandfather of Noah. Enoch was known as a highly virtuous man who walked with God. His Hebrew name was *Henoch* which signifies *"to initiate and to instruct,"* Masonic scholars believe that Enoch introduced the speculative principles into the Masonic creed and that he originated its exclusive character. He spent his living days on and around Mt. Moriah in Jerusalem. Enoch was inspired by the Most High to build an under ground temple and dedicate it to God. His son, Methuselah, actually built and finished the unique temple which consisted of nine vaults placed perpendicularly on top of one another. The openings in each vault were arch shaped. Enoch created a cubit (17 to 21 inches) long triangular plate of gold on which he engraved the ineffable characters and true name of Deity and then placed the engraved plate on a pedestal in the bottom vault. After depositing the golden plate, a stone door was placed over the upper vault to hide the entrance and prevent its discovery. Enoch then constructed one architectural column of brass and another of marble. On the brass pillar, he inscribed the history of creation, the principle of arts and sciences and the doctrines of Speculative Freemasonry as it was practiced in his lifetime. On the marble pillar he inscribed characters in hieroglyphics which implied that a treasure was buried in a subterranean vault nearby. Enoch passed away in 987 with hope that the vault would be found by someone who would someday build a temple dedicated to Jehovah on Mt. Moriah. King Solomon later came and built God's temple on the mountain. (Encyclopedia of Freemasonry by Albert G. Mackey, 33o M.D.)

THE FIRST SITE ... A CHURCH
COLONY BEGINS

A newly organized Mormon colony moved from upper New York to Kirtland, Ohio, in 1831 where they established their first church headquarters. Kirtland was located at what is now the eastern edge of the Cleveland Metropolitan Area and a few short miles south of Lake Erie. Sidney Rigdon, a Cambellite[5] minister, arrived and joined the new church

---

[5] Cambellite was the title given to a "spinoff" group of Baptist who followed the movement of a religious reformer named Alexander Cambell. Sidney Rigdon was an ordained Baptist minister who had been preaching as a Philadelphia Regular Baptist, first adhering to the Calvinist tenets, but he then accepted the Cambell emphasis that the New Testament was the true Gospel. Rigdon

in Kirtland. He was immediately elevated into the church leadership because of his theological background. Sidney Rigdon brought with him hundreds of his Restorationist followers who all converted to the new Church of Christ. The new church name was then changed to the "Church of the Latter-day Saints," after which the leadership hierarchy was refined to create the High Council of Zion or *Quorum of the Twelve Apostles*. Sidney Rigdon went right to work to help Prophet Smith produce a new Biblical translation for the <u>Book of Genesis</u> and for the New Testament.

As this new religious community grew, the first Mormon temple was erected in which many important church doctrines were established such as: . . . the early version of the ordained member endowment, foot washing, Solemn Assembly, School of Prophets, Word of Wisdom (to involve advocating temperance), dietary restrictions, and the launch of plural marriage. The Mormon religious ritual and liturgy became well formed and established in Kirtland. It was there that Prophet Joseph Smith married his first plural wife, Fanny Alger, in 1833. The Prophet was to have 33 plural wives during his lifetime and to include Lucinda, the young widow of Captain William Morgan. Kirtland Latter-day Saints were heavily encouraged to consider moving west to a new City of Zion being established in Missouri. The City of Zion was being built near the Kansas City Area and was designated as the location for the true second coming of Christ.

Prophet Joseph Smith and Sydney Rigdon created a bank in Kirtland in 1837 to serve their growing church community.

---

insisted that baptism was for the remission of sins which was contrary to the Regular Baptist's understanding. Joseph Smith sot out Sidney Rigdon based on the factor that their theological ideas were much the same. Sidney Rigdon was an outstanding orator and served in the key oratorical position for Joseph Smith.

The bank soon failed and disillusioned some 300 of the church membership. Church leaders joined with many bank customers who felt that they had been personally violated. The new Mormon Church leaders then took control of the temple and formally excommunicated young Prophet Smith and Rigdon. In 1838, Prophet Smith managed to successfully escape many death threats in Kirtland by safely hiding inside a wooden coffin for a secret ride out of town. Prophet Smith and Sidney Rigdon both headed for the town of Far West located in Jackson County, Missouri, and which was the town for their Western Mormon Outpost. Many loyal followers also left Kirtland and joined the church movement in Missouri.

MISTAKEN VISION ... THE CITY OF ZION

The Latter-day Saints settled east of Independence, Missouri, in the Jackson County area. Newly arriving Mormon settlers were directed to participate in constructing the City of Zion buildings and homes in preparation for the second coming of Jesus. This settlement did grow rapidly but the rapid Mormon settlement growth incited a revolt among the local citizens. Non-Mormon citizens in the area felt that the expanding Mormon settlement was beginning to dominate both the direction and control in all local government. The citizens became afraid that they would lose political power and fought back in 1833 by using local vigilantes who did succeed in driving the Mormons out of Jackson County. All Mormon followers living in that county abruptly lost their homes and most of their personal property. The Mormon survivors then moved and settled in nearby Clay County.

The Mormons pleaded with Jackson County officials in an attempt to regain their lost personal properties but all efforts failed. During this time, new converts to Mormonism continued to migrate to Missouri and settle into the Clay County colony near the town of Far West.

The Missouri legislature, in sympathy with the settlers, created Caldwell County in 1836 to provide a specific area to serve the Mormon settlement. Caldwell county was located more northeast of the Kansas City Metropolitan Area. A short time later, Prophet Smith and Sidney Rigdon reached Caldwell County where they regained their church stature. Soon after their arrival, a political power struggle occurred among the Missouri Latter-day Saint leaders. Church leaders David Whitmer, Oliver Cowdry, William Wines Phelps and others were formally excommunicated from the Latter-day Saints movement, for just cause, and they proceeded to form their own Mormon Church which became known as the Whitmerite Schism of the Latter-day Saints. The Whitmerites chose to develop their church under the name: "Church of Christ."

The church and its mission continued to expand in Missouri resulting in another name change to become: "Church of Jesus Christ of Latter-day Saints." Shortly after this name change, the "Law of Tithing" was established within the movement. The Mormons began to expand and plant more colonies in areas surrounding Caldwell County. This expansion created new friction between the non-Mormon settlers and the Mormons. Locals felt that Mormons were too preoccupied with their own people and were not at all friendly with the area settlers, and the settlers did not respect the evidence of polygamy in the colony. The Mormons again tended to take dominating control of the county government. The hefty Mormon population took on a militant stand which triggered the 1838 Mormon War. As a result of their rebellious militant attitude, some Mormon leaders including Thomas B. Marsh, president of the Quorum of Twelve Apostles, broke away from Prophet Smith and Rigdon to create yet another Latter-day Saints schism. This schism led to the formation of the "Church of Jesus Christ, the Bride, the Lamb's Wife" under the leadership of George M. Hinkle who had served in Caldwell County as a Missouri Militia Commander. The Mormon War then escalated throughout the county. In retaliation, the State of Missouri sent out 2,500 militia troops to put down the "Mormon Rebellion" and forcefully drive the Mormons out of the state. It was feared that the Mormon settlers would likely be massacred and Colonel George Hinkle arranged the arrest of Prophet Smith and other church leaders in an effort to prevent a massacre. The leaders were incarcerated in a Liberty, Missouri, jail. The Latter-day Saints followers again lost their properties and were expelled from Missouri by a directive of the Missouri Governor. The displaced Mormons now looked for a new place to settle and live in peace. They headed northeast to Iowa and Illinois.

SAFE ESCAPE TO ILLINOIS...
A NEW PLACE TO BEGIN

Displaced Latter-day Saint refugees reached the Illinois border by 1839 and were met by friendly Quincy, Illinois, citizens who welcomed them and offered help and assistance. Soon after arriving in Illinois, the Mormons searched and found land on the Illinois bank of the Mississippi River above Quincy, borrowed money and purchased the abandoned town of Commerce, Illinois. The Mormons named the newly acquired town: Nauvoo ("Beautiful Place" in Hebrew). Back in Missouri, and after several months of rough jail treatment, Prophet Smith and other church leaders were allowed to escape custody. They traveled to Illinois and rejoined their colony.

The new land purchased in Illinois suffered with environmental problems. The land was in a mosquito infested wet land at a bend in the Mississippi River. The followers worked to install canals and drain the soil to make the riverside flatland habitable. The local governments encouraged the Latter-day Saints to establish their Illinois colony and granted them a wide degree of autonomy. The Mormons were then granted a charter by the state that authorized setting up their own independent municipal courts. They were also granted full freedom to establish a university plus an authorization to organize their own Nauvoo militia. One of the first colony priorities in 1841 was to build a Latter-day Saints temple on the hilltop overlooking the Nauvoo commerce center.

With deep reflection, Prophet Smith truly marveled at how the vision for his movement was coming together in Nauvoo. Prophet Smith now formally established himself as the Prophet and leader of the Mormon Church colony. He proceeded to finalized a few more Mormon practices during the days and months that followed. Baptism for the dead was introduced, as well as Rebaptism from Other Faiths, the Nauvoo-era Endowment, and the Ordinance for the Second Anointing. Additionally, he created a new inner church council, which included both men and women and became known as the "Anointed Quorum." At this point, and since Prophet Smith had been participating in plural marriage, he formally introduced plural marriage as a doctrine to be included in the Church discipline and used by all followers. Plural marriage became an attraction for adding new converts to the colony.

The colony grew rapidly as a result of overwhelming response to invitations sent out to domestic and foreign destinations that invited families and businesses to the colony. Many industriously talented people arrived and contributed efficiency and productiveness to the Mormon colony. Notable and talented people from the British Isles and Eastern United States settled in Nauvoo and did become part of the Latter-day Saints movement. A population growth rose to 12,000 residents at Nauvoo's peak size. The population growth was also the result of implementing the practice of plural wives, which was a positive method for rapidly expanding all colony families. At that same time, Chicago, Illinois, (later to become the second largest city in the United States) had reached a population of 15,000 people. Notable people throughout Illinois recognized this growing Western Illinois community and talk started relative to making Nauvoo the new state capital.

One notable person who was attracted to the colony was Jonathan Browning, a skilled gunsmith. Jonathan Browning and his family were originally from Tennessee and had relocated to Quincy, Illinois. He was convinced to leave Quincy, Illinois, shortly after he had invented the sliding breach "Harmonica gun."[6] He and his family moved to Nauvoo and joined the colony. He built a small cabin with part as a home and part as a gunsmith shop so that he could care for his family and work at his trade. Jonathan Browning continued making his gunsmith success by creating new rifle innovations and new gun manufacturing methods while living in Nauvoo. He and his family later departed along with the Nauvoo Mormons as they migrated west and camped at Kanesville, Iowa, a major stopping point on the migration trail to Salt Lake City. Browning was asked to stay in Kanesville for a time and be a gunsmith to assist migrants for their trip west. After a brief stay, Jonathan

---

[6] The Harmonica gun was made to use a flat horizontal magazine (slide) that was engaged through the pistol and/or gun breech. The magazine was moved manually to advance and load chambers. The name came from the gun magazine that looked like a horizontal harmonica.

Browning migrated with other Mormons to Salt Lake City but be he then moved and settled his family in Ogden, Utah. It was in Ogden, Utah, that his famous inventor son, John Moses Browning, was born. Jonathan Browning was a polygamist in his personal life and he supported three wives and nineteen children. In addition to Jonathan Browning, many notable business owners joined the Nauvoo colony and their contributions and identity can be found in the well kept Nauvoo historical records.

John Browning Gunsmith Shop and Home

NAUVOO MASONIC LODGE...
ALL MORMON MEN BECOME MASONS

Masonry came to Illinois in 1835 when the Grand Lodge of Kentucky issued a dispensation to Masons living in Quincy, Illinois, to form Bodley Masonic Lodge No. 97. Members of this new lodge then curiously searched throughout Illinois to learn the number of Masons who had settled within the state. Six Masonic Lodges were found functioning and each had a dispensation originating in another state. On April 28, 1840 representatives from these six lodges met in Jacksonville, Illinois, and unanimously resolved to form an Illinois Grand Lodge. During the election of their Grand Lodge officers, Abraham Jonas was selected as the Most Worshipful Grand Master. When the Illinois Grand Lodge, Ancient Free & Accepted Masons, had been incorporated,

Bodley Lodge and the other five lodges cancelled their out-of-state charters and assumed new charters under the Grand Lodge of Illinois. New assumed lodge identities became: Bodley Lodge No. 1, Quincy; Equality Lodge No. 2, Equality; Harmony Lodge No. 3, Jacksonville; Springfield Lodge No. 4, Springfield; Far West Lodge No. 5, Galena (This Lodge never met and vacated their charter, but they later became Far West Lodge No. 41 in 1846.); Columbus Lodge No. 6, Columbus (This Lodge vacated in 1845).

Freemasonry was known among the Latter-day Saints because most of the original Latter-day Saints' founders had become Freemasons in states where they once lived: Joseph Smith, Sr, Hyrum Smith, Heber Kimball, Elijah Fordam, Newel Whitney, James Adams, and John Bennett. Each of these men had been motivated to join Freemasonry by the influence of American Revolutionary Patriots such as Benjamin Franklin, George Washington and eight signers of the Declaration of Independence.

John Bennett, one of the founders living in Nauvoo, had become a better known participant in Illinois Freemasonry and he applied to the Most Worshipful Grand Master of Illinois for permission to establish a Masonic Lodge in Nauvoo. On March 15, 1842 the Illinois Grand Lodge traveled to, and met in Nauvoo. This meeting resulted in the Nauvoo Rising Sun Lodge of Freemasons becoming established by Abraham Jonas, the Most Worshipful Illinois Grand Master. Masons from the Quincy Bodley Lodge assisted in instituting the new lodge. It was interesting that Prophet Joseph Smith actually sat in and served as Grand Chaplain during this meeting even though he was not yet a Mason. That evening, Prophet Smith received his first degree (Entered Apprentice) and the following day he was initiated into the Second and Third Degree (Master Mason) *"at sight"* by Worshipful Grand Master Jonas. The initiation of a deserving free man *"at sight"* was fully within Worshipful Grand Master Jonas' authority, but membership sanctioning *"at sight"* is a fairly rare occurrence (*"at sight"* means acting on the instant word of the Grand Master which provides complete membership without a formal ritualistic presentation, or the need for the candidate to commit the Masonic Catechism to memory). On the same day, Sidney Rigdon was also made a Master Mason *"at sight"* by Illinois Worshipful Grand Master Jonas. On the day after becoming a Master Mason, Prophet Smith personally established a female relief society to include women who would function in all likeness to the Masonic Order. Among Prophet Smith's instructions to the sisters were such words as: "Each must adhere to ancient orders; examinations; degrees; candidates; secrets; lodges; rules; signs and priesthoods" all of which indicated influences that were found in Freemasonry."

In only a few months after the Nauvoo Rising Sun Lodge began holding regular lodge meetings, 286 new members had been initiated into the lodge as Master Masons. Members of Bodley Lodge No. 1 in Quincy became suspicious of the almost instant rise in lodge membership and questioned the Illinois Grand Lodge about the special dispensation granted to establish the Nauvoo Lodge. Many lodge operating irregularities were reported to the Grand Lodge by Brodley Lodge members who had observed that the Nauvoo Rising Sun Lodge protocol was contrary to Masonic ritual and disciplines. Some examples of misconduct reported were instances where: the Nauvoo lodge combined submitted candidate petitions and voted on them collectively rather than voting on each petition separately; each degree was conferred upon a group of candidates rather than one candidate at a time; and all three degrees were actually conferred within the same day or week rather than being spaced with the stipulated thirty days separation between degree presentations. An investigation into the Nauvoo

Lodge irregularities resulted in suspending the Nauvoo Lodge in August 1842—"for just reason," and the suspension remained in place until the Illinois Grand Lodge met for their annual meeting in October 1842. During the brief time that the Nauvoo Lodge had been in operation, John Bennett reported one instance when sixty-three petitioners were elected on one ballot. In normal Masonic protocol only one candidate was to be voted on and elected at a time and only a single candidate was to be taken through each of three degrees at any one time. Also, there was a mandatory 30 day minimum separation in time between each of the three degree presentations to allow the initiate time to memorize and recite the degree catechism from memory. However, the Illinois Grand Lodge later lifted their suspension and allowed the Nauvoo Lodge to resume its operation. Masonry flourished well among the Mormons to the extent that additional Mormon Masonic Lodges were chartered. Regardless of the brief Grand Lodge suspension, the several operating irregularities seemed to continue. Every eligible Mormon male became initiated into Freemasonry through the Nauvoo lodges. The Masonic membership in Nauvoo grew dramatically in a surprising short time to reach near a total of 1500 Mormon Masons. During that same time, by comparison, there were only 250 Masonic members counted in all the rest of Illinois. In 1843, the Illinois Grand Lodge shut down all five Mormon Lodges because of their deviation from Masonic discipline and ordered them to cease any and all Masonic work.

On April 5, 1844, one year after the Illinois Grand Lodge shut down all Mormon Masonic Lodges, the new Nauvoo Masonic Temple building was completed and dedicated. This building was the largest building in Nauvoo aside from the temple that was under construction. The Mormons ignored the Illinois Grand Lodge order to stop all Masonic operations and continued to function as deceptive clandestine lodges.

The Latter-day Saints used the new Masonic Temple for both clandestine Masonic meetings and to conduct church endowment ceremonies. The endowment ceremony and other sacred rites were later moved to the partially finished Latter-day Saints Temple in the winter of 1845-1846.

Masonic ritual and principals apparently influenced Prophet Smith as he developed his new Latter-day Saints disciplines. Two months after Prophet Smith was made a Master Mason he presented a new *Ordained Endowment* to the Mormon Masons. Newly Endowed Mormon Masons did perceive similarities with the Masonic ritual in the new church ritual. Some similarities could be identified with the beginning of the first, second and third Masonic degrees. However, just the standard three basic Masonic Symbolic Lodge degrees had been presented to new Mormon Masons. The Mormon Masons had not experienced the unique Royal Arch portion of Ancient Masonic work exposed in William Morgan's *"Illustrations of Masonry,"* and which once was part of the basic Freemason initiation. The new candidates had not witnessed, nor could they know that portions of the *endowment* mirrored the Royal Arch degree ritual. The Royal Arch of Solomon degree had been separated from the symbolic three Masonic degrees back in 1813 and relocated into advanced Masonic ritual as the Thirteenth Degree in the Ancient Accepted Scottish Rite and into York Rite ritual as the Royal Arch of Zerubbabel.

As Freemasons learned more about the Mormon religion they became severally disturbed as they began to recognize their secret Masonic ritual entwined in the Mormon ritual. To all Freemasons the long history of the Masonry is hallowed and dates back to a beginning during the building of King

Solomon' temple. In that history, King Solomon[7] built his temple by God's direction for the purpose of giving and granting endowments for special circumstances, but King Solomon actually granted but few, if any actual endowments

---

[7] Here is a historic reflection of King Solomon as scholars relate: . . . King Solomon built and dedicated his temple to God using stone masons and craftsmen under the architect Hiram Abif, also known as the "Widow's Son". Solomon's friend, Hiram, King of Tyre sent Hiram Abif to King Solomon to direct all temple work. The "Widow's Son" was a title used because Hiram's original father had died when he was a young man, but his mother later married another man of Tyre. His father of Tyre taught Hiram a wide range of building trade skills. His father was highly accomplished in all building construction methods from stone and metal to wood and he was often identified as a unique artisan. He was regularly drawn into service by King Solomon because of his successful building skills. King Solomon was satisfied with Hiram Abif supervising all work during the temple construction. Hiram, King of Tyre supplied some 33,600 craftsmen builders from Tyre to build the temple. The craftsmen were organized into a pattern of authority which consisted of Grand Masters and Grand Wardens who directed specific areas of the temple work. A "chain of command" by the Masters and Wardens established a special discipline, reverence, and respect among all workers. Hiram Abif daily offered prayer in the temple confines at the rising sun and at the setting sun. At noonday sun, he would inspect all work. The craftsmen completed a large, perfectly constructed, beautiful and ornate temple in the span of seven years. Hiram Abif abruptly died, disrespectfully, just before the ceremony for the temple completion. Through the years following the completion of King Solomon's Temple, the craftsmen and masons maintained the Master and Warden structure along with their special reverence and disciplines by forming craftsmen guilds. The Masonic Order after King Solomon's time often became restructured from its origin until it developed into what we now see after the year 1717. (See Kings I, 8:13-14; Chronicles II, 2:13-14.)

during his 40 year reign as king. From the Nauvoo beginning, the Latter-day Saints *endowed* each and every new church member candidate with their secret temple ceremony as each candidate entered into Mormon Sainthood. As the Masonic ritual is secret except to its Masonic members, we find that the *endowment* is a ritual that is secret in the Mormon Church and only for its members. (Today, by virtue of the computer internet, many of both Masonic and Mormon rituals can be viewed and compared.)

Some similarities were recognized between the Masonic degrees and the Mormon *endowment,* the Mormons clothed each endowment candidate in a white robe for a purification ceremony, a procedure which also occurred in the Royal Arch of Solomon degree in Masonry. In addition to the white robe, each Mormon candidate was also clothed in an undergarment that Prophet Smith had developed for all of the saints. Each candidate was dressed in a special snug fitting white underclothing that was worn during the *endowment* ceremony and thereafter throughout the saint's faithful life. Each endowed saint is taught that the undergarment "shields and protects him from harm." This garment was arrayed with special embroidered symbols that were alluded to during the endowment ceremony such as a "Λ" (points of a compass) on the left breast and an "L" (square) on the right breast. There was also found a horizontal line across the navel as symbolic of the evisceration penalty for disclosing Mormon secrets and a slash to expose a naked right knee. (The embroidered symbology mirrors symbols physically used by Masons during their Masonic degrees.) Each *endowment* candidate was to assume the new name of "Enoch."

When a Masonic candidate was presented in the (Ancient) Royal Arch Degree, he was clothed in a plain white rob only when and as the degree was administered. The following sample Masonic degree verbiage is presented to compare with some of the verbiage extracted from the Endowment Ceremony:

The Endowment Ceremony is believed to be copied and reworded, for the most part, from Captain William Morgan's book. When comparing the early Endowment Ceremony to the Masonic ritual, we find stark similarities to the degrees in Freemasonry. The following representative examples show these similarities:

Mormon Text: "We, and each of us, covenant and promise that we will not reveal any of the secrets of this, the first token of the Aaronic priesthood, with its accompanying name, sign or penalty. Should we do so, we agree that our throats be cut from ear to ear and our tongues torn out by their roots . . ." (W.M. Paden, Temple Mormonism, 1931, p. 18)

Mason Text: "I . . . will never reveal any part or parts, arts or arts, point or points of the secret arts and mysteries of ancient Freemasonry . . . binding myself under a no less penalty than to have my throat cut across, my tongue torn out by the roots . . ." (William Morgan, Illustrations of Masonry, 1827, pp. 21-22)

Compare the Second Token of the Aaronic Priesthood with the Second Degree Masonic oath:

Mormon Text: "We and each of us do covenant and promise that we will not reveal the secrets of this, the Second Token of Aaronic Priesthood, with its accompanying name, sign, grip, or penalty. Should we do so, we agree to have our breasts cut open and our hearts and vitals torn from our bodies and given to the birds of the air and beasts of the field." (Paden, p. 20)

Masonic Text: "I . . . most solemnly and sincerely promise and swear . . . that I will not give the degree of a Fellow Craft Mason to one of an inferior degree, nor any other being of the known world . . . binding myself under no less penalty than to have my left breast torn open and my heart and vitals taken from thence . . . to become a prey to the beasts of the field, and vultures in the air . . ." (Morgan, Illustrations of Masonry, p. 52)

Besides similar penalties, there are similar signs, arm positions, ear whisperings, passwords and handgrips. For instance "The First token of Aaronic Priesthood" grip is compared with the "First Degree" Masonic grip:

Mormon Text:

Peter—"What is that?"

Adam—"The first token of the Aaronic Priesthood."

Peter—"Has it a name?"

Adam—"It has."

Peter—"Will you give it to me?"

Adam—"I can not, for it is connected with my new name, but this is the sign" (Paden, p. 20)

Masonic Text:

"What is this?"

Ans. "A grip."

"A grip of what?"

Ans. "The grip of an Entered Apprentice Mason."

"Has it a name?"

Ans. "It has."

"Will you give it to me?"

Ans. "I did not so receive it, neither can I so impart it." (Morgan, pp. 23-24)

(It should be noted that the Latter Day Saints Endowment Ceremony has recently undergone changes that depart from the original Endowment.)

DEATH OF THE PROPHET!...
WHAT HAPPENS NEXT?

By 1844, neighbors living around Nauvoo felt that the growing Mormon population was gradually taking a dominant control over the politics for the region. In contention was a growing rivalry for the commercial development in Hancock County. Among the area natives, the Mormon religion was, in fact, terribly different from the Protestant and Catholic churches which had been long established throughout the area. Then there was a moral issue directed at the colony's adherence to polygamy. The loss of available women became a special disturbance to the young men who had found that most all of the eligible single women had been taken as multiple wives for the Mormon men. And, basically, the Mormons did not feel any obligation to follow the established local conventions and preferred to dominate and establish their own doctrines, practices and government.

In March 1844, Prophet Smith held a very private meeting to organize the Secret Council of the Kingdom. Proceedings in this meeting proclaimed Prophet Smith as Prophet, Priest, and King as well as fully re-endorsing the doctrine of polygamy. The *Nauvoo Expositor Newspaper* learned about these secret proclamations and threatened to publically release details. Smith, acting as mayor and head of the municipal court responded by declaring Marshall Law and declared the newspaper a public nuisance. He ordered the newspaper's immediate destruction. By the hands of colony men, the newspaper's printing presses were smashed and Prophet Smith's full mandate was carried out. Non-Mormons throughout the state clamored for Prophet Smith's arrest because of his malicious judgment and unconstitutional action against the newspaper. A new anti-Mormon resentment quickly resulted from border to border in Hancock County and beyond.

Illinois Governor Thomas Ford was made aware of the Nauvoo issues and traveled to Hancock County to investigate the uprising. At that time Prophet Smith was officiating as the Mayor of Nauvoo and he was also running as a candidate for the presidency of the United States. On June 25, 1844, Prophet Smith, his brother, Hyrum Smith, three church associates and fifteen city council members, surrendered themselves to Governor Ford to admit to the revengeful action they had taken with the newspaper. Their surrender was their personal hope to gain protection from the aroused anti-Mormon mob. Prophet Smith and the group of men were arrested and taken to the nearby Carthage Jail. As soon as Prophet Smith and Hyrum Smith arrived at the jail, they both were charged with treason against the State of Illinois for declaring martial law in Nauvoo. Both brothers, along with their three Mormon associates, were held for trial. The fifteen city council members were released on bonds. Governor Ford then abruptly departed Carthage to return to Nauvoo and took the primary jail officials with him leaving only three "Carthage Grey" anti-Mormon militia to guard the prisoners. A friend visiting Prophet Smith earlier that day had handed the Prophet a small pepper-box pistol in case he might be need some personal protection.

On the afternoon of June 27, 1844, excited anti-Mormon citizens, wearing gunpowder blackened faces, marched on the jail and began to frenzy. Prophet Smith did not worry about the advancing mob because he thought the mob was actually the Nauvoo Legion coming to rescue him. The mob rushed the jail and crowded to the up stair cells to kill both Prophet Smith and Hyrum Smith. Hyrum was instantly shot and killed. Prophet Smith's pepper-box pistol misfired but he was able to fire three shots that hit attackers. The prophet dashed to escape through an upper story window. As he flew through the window he was shot twice in the back and once from the ground. He could be heard exclaiming: *"Oh Lord, my God, ". . .* as his body fell to the ground. He never lived an instant longer to complete the (Masonic) distress signal and words: *". . . is there no help for the Widow's Son?"* The three associates were shot at but escaped from both the jail and crowd. Both dead brothers were found to be "naked," meaning they were not wearing their Latter-day Saints undergarments which meant that they were baring their souls for sins they felt responsible for. Fellow Mormons then claimed the two bodies and saw to their proper funeral and burial. Precautions were taken during and following the funeral to insure that neither body was stolen. The bodies were buried securely in Nauvoo.

Some of the men among the attacking mob were suspected to have been Masons. Five men involved in the murders were identified and legally tried by a jury in a court of law, but all were later acquitted after the prosecuting attorney and judge ruled in favor of the men. One defendant, Thomas Sharp, had been the chosen leader of the local Anti-Mormon Movement. Thomas Sharp was the editor for the City of Warsaw newspaper in which he had published stories decrying the Mormons. After being acquitted in the trial, Thomas Sharp joined with two other defendants, Jacob Davis and Levi Williams, and fled to the Warsaw Masonic Lodge No. 21 (chartered in January 1843) where they hoped to hide and re-establish their esteem in the community. All three men wanted to become Masons to further win favor with their friends and neighbors. The three did begin their initiation into the Warsaw Lodge between October and December 1844. Illinois Grand Lodge officers became aware of what was happening at the Warsaw Lodge and called for an investigation. The matter was brought before the annual Grand Lodge meeting in 1845 and the Warsaw Lodge was found guilty of violating Masonic regulations. Warsaw Lodge soon thereafter dissolved to save face.

A new crisis was now eminent for the colony. A Mormon succession crisis became the immediate challenge to the *Quorum of Twelve Apostles*. Hyrum, had been next in the succession line but he was now dead. The second-in-line, Brother Samuel Smith, died a month later. The *Quorum of Twelve Apostles* then became temporarily headed by Brigham Young. Brigham Young was Prophet Smith's neighbor and his close associate in the Quorum of Twelve. Brigham Young was later officially selected to assume the LDS leadership. William Marks, presiding high council for Nauvoo LDS, and Sidney Rigdon who had been excommunicated when Joseph Smith was the highest executive in the Quorum, both vied for ultimate leadership in the church but such consideration was denied. The *Quorum of Twelve Apostles* was re-authorized and established as the official presiding Latter-day Saints authority. Further battles for the church leadership continued for a short time but all action remained strictly on the sidelines and never officially overtook the direction of the Latter-day Saints members.

While the LDS leadership crisis was being solved, the momentum created by the Illinois Mormon War was generating into a near disaster. Mormon properties were being looted and burned. Latter-day Saints living outside and around Nauvoo were forced to move into Nauvoo for their own protection. Many did not want to follow the colony and relocate to the proposed Utah Territory. New schisms started occurring where those who felt they were true leaders in their own right pulled away from the central church and formed their own church and then headed out to new destinations.

On April 11, 1845 Brigham Young ordered that all clandestine Mormon Masonic Lodge meetings in Nauvoo be discontinued. This was a year after the Illinois Grand Lodge had formally shut down all Nauvoo lodges. Some Mormon Masons did cross over the Mississippi and were welcomed at Masonic Lodge meetings in Montrose, Iowa.

In October 1845 the anti-Mormon people in and around Quincy met as the "Quincy Convention" and in their diligence leveled resolutions demanding that the Mormons living in the Nauvoo area must vacate the Illinois territory by May 1846. Citizens of Carthage organized the Carthage Militia to enforce the exodus of the Mormon population out of Illinois.

Preparations to leave Nauvoo started in 1845 after Brigham Young announced that the LDS Mormons would abandon Illinois beginning in the spring of 1846. In his announcement Brigham Young proclaimed: *"We leave when water flows and grass grows; we will be heading west to the Utah Territory"*.

Reflecting back a few years prior, Prophet Smith had had a perception that he would one day build a kingdom in a place of beauty located somewhere in the Rocky Mountains. The location would be where there would be no interference with his new religious movement. His vision was now becoming reality. All colony efforts focused on preparing for a mass westward departure. As frantic preparations were in progress even the senior women, those who were not involved with daily commerce and who normally attended to child care and home chores, were pressed into service to whittle and assemble small parts used in the wagon wheel hubs. Notably, all cargo wagons were built to one single plan so that each wagon contained like parts that could be swapped out to save a wagon during a breakdown on the westward trail. Extra iron shoes were made for the cloven hove oxen pulling the wagons. Each family packed only what personal items would fit in the wagons in addition to abundant provisions for the long overland journey.

Brutal local mob actions arose again all around Nauvoo and fighting became destructively vicious. Mormons were beaten and there homes burned. The state of Illinois leaders had become concerned that the Mormons were becoming far too powerful and feared that they would grow unfavorably in political power and overtake the state government. Masons feared that the new member growth in Mormon Masons could overtake the Illinois Grand Lodge structure. Young anti-Mormon men in the area were terribly distraught about losing the large bulk of available women to court. Mormons still living outside of Nauvoo were getting scared as they saw killings rise and felt forced to somehow escape from the area. An urgent decision was made to make an earlier departure on February 4, 1846. Wagons began immediately crossing the Mississippi River to Iowa. Chaos did prevail among the departing Mormons and caused some to leave without receiving the ordained *endowment* in their new temple. All those who deeply desired the special ceremony and blessing hesitated in Iowa and re-crossed the river during the night to achieve the *endowment* before setting out. Since it was winter, some departing families had a remote hope that the Mississippi River width would freeze hard enough to support crossing wagons, but such did not happen. Ice jams did occur from time-to-time which did allow some foot traffic across the river. Residents from Quincy, Illinois came up river and helped the masses to leave. Local flat bed ferries operated between Illinois and Iowa to move wagons, livestock and people across the frigid river. The main core of migrants encamped at a place denoted as Sugar Creek Camp on the Iowa side of the river to better prepare for the riggers of winter before starting their trip west.

Emma Hale Smith, Prophet Smith's wife, and her children remained behind in Nauvoo after the mass migration departed. In 1860, her eldest Smith son, Joseph Smith III claimed that he received a revelation calling him to take the place of his prophet father and become president of a "new organization" of the Latter-day Saint Church which planned to remain in the Midwest. These Midwestern remnants came together as the *Reorganized Church of Jesus Christ of Latter-day Saints,* now called *the Community of Christ.* This group became the second largest Latter-day Saints group and later relocated to Independence, Missouri.

NEW FREEDOM ... THE LARGEST MIGRATION IN U.S. HISTORY

The westward movement proceeded along a previously traveled trail that now became identified as the "Mormon Trail." This trail intertwined with a westerly "Oregon–California Trail". Mormon migrants joined other settlers heading west on the intertwined trails. Indians granted safe passage usually in exchange for coffee and food staples. At times, a unit of livestock was relinquished to Indians to insure safe passage. Normally, peace prevailed between the travelers and Indians but there were some random rogue Indian hostilities. This trek spanned 1300 miles and has been recorded as the largest mass migration recorded in United States history.

The Iowa segment of the migration was severely taxing on the inexperienced travelers. Constant rain fell and deep mud kept the wagon wheels half buried. Most of the travelers had not traveled long distances over land and most had not adequately provisioned themselves for the trip. A major stop was made by the group on the west side of the Missouri River and became an encampment they named, "Winter Quarters" (this camp later became Omaha, Nebraska). Other groups stopped on the east side of the Missouri river at a new town named "Kanesville." Kanesville was named for Thomas L. Kane who had succeeded in getting federal permission for the Mormons to camp on Indian land from 1846-1847 (Kanesville later became Council Bluff in 1852). While at the "Winter Quarters," the Mormons became better organized and then re-provisioned to launch their travel west now in groups or organized companies. Many headed out in wagon trains accompanied by militia members such as the Vanguard Company and the Mormon Battalion. The trek west from "Winter Quarters" went better after the migrants had honed their skills to handle the next rugged travel distance.

Mormon Masons often confronted Master Mason Brigham Young about Masonry as the group migrated west. Understand, too, that all the eligible Mormon men had become Masons prior to setting out on this trip. They brought up numerous questions regarding the similarity between the Mormon *endowment* ceremony and the Freemason ritual. Many Mormons believed that Freemasonry had evolved as a result of the *endowment* ceremony. Brigham Young responded as best he was able that the *endowment* ceremony and Freemasonry were definitely different and unique from one another. As soon as the migrants arrived and settled in Salt Lake City, all the men were instantly put to work constructing their own homes and building necessary city buildings. All their time was consumed by long hours of demanding work. This was planned to keep everyone totally occupied and especially to keep their minds off the questions of *endowment* similarities with Freemasonry. In the mean time, Brigham Young wrote to the Grand Lodge of England and requested that the Latter-day Saints be permitted to form their own Masonic lodge and that they be allowed to structure lodge proceedings in line with Latter-day Saints ideas. This request was flatly rejected. Brigham Young then proceeded to keep all men busy so that their minds were absorbed in the immediate community necessities and oblivious to thoughts of Freemasonry. No Masonic lodges had been established in the Utah Territory when the Latter-day Saints initially arrived in 1847, nor would there be any Masonry for another ten years.

Brigham Young and his Mormon associates formally established the Great Salt Lake City in 1847 (In 1858, the word: "Great" was removed from the city title.). The Quorum of Twelve firmly believed that they had finally found their "Zion," and a place where their new religion would be free from outside interference. Brigham Young became territorial governor and led his following well. In 1857, United States President James Buchanan received a message from a federal judge in the Utah territory suggesting that an insurrection or rebellion by the LDS was occurring. The president dispatched Johnston's Army of 1,500 federal troops to suppress what was thought to be a Latter-day Saints rebellion. When word reached Governor Brigham Young that federal troops were in route on a mission to incarcerate or kill all the Latter-day Saints, he dispatched militia patrols into the territory and sent special forces into Emigrant Canyon to intercept and deal with all incoming military.

Brigham Young sent word to all Mormon settlements in the territory advising them that war on the Mormon colonies was now evident. All Mormon settlers were advised to pack up and head back to Salt Lake City. The arid September 1857 desert and the extreme overland distances made communications with his southern contingents undependable. When an advisory was received, it did create hysteria and Mormons reacted in fear of another war. In the southern area, six days distant and directly south of Salt Lake City, the Nauvoo Legion militia mobilized under fearful concerns for the safety of the settlements. The militia designed plans to attack the Baker-Fancher party who was encamped in the Mountain Meadow Area along the Old Spanish Trail. The Baker-Fancher wagon train had originated in Arkansas and made a stop in Salt Lake City when they chose to follow the Old Spanish Trail south from Salt Lake City. The southern Mormons in Parowan and Cedar City suspected that some members of the Baker-Fancher party had poisoned a spring near Corn Creek which resulted in killing eighteen cows and three people. Answering to their suspicions and fear, the Mormons convinced some Southern Paiute Indians to join them in the attack on the encamped wagon train and make it look like an Indian assault. Governor Brigham Young received word of what the militia contemplated and immediately sent back a rider with a letter stating that the Baker-Fancher party was not to be meddled with. As the rider was dispatched from Salt Lake City, members of the Mormon Legion had disguised themselves as Indians and joined the Paiute to lay siege on the wagon train for five days. Some of the migrants recognized white men among the attackers. Out of fear of being connected to the attack, Legion members resumed dress as settlers and approached the wagon train under a flag of truce and spirited the surviving migrants away to a secluded place where they murdered them. All 120 adults were massacred but the legion left the infant children unharmed. The surviving children were given to local Mormon families. Remnants of the wagon train were sold at auction. The massacre was made to look like the

Indians had been the sole culprit. The Mormon leaders of the attack were pursued and some went to court. Some were excommunicated from the church. Major John D. Lee was tried, prosecuted and shot by firing squad for his leadership involvement.

When the approaching federal troops learned about the Mormon defensive measures, Colonel Leiper, who had earlier befriended some of the Mormon's, entered from the southern part of the territory and asked for a meeting with Brigham Young. A meeting was successfully held and Colonel Leiper convinced Brigham Young that the army's purpose was not to destroy the Saints but that the army was there to peacefully install governmental power to the region, establish needed control of the Indians and regulate emigrant travel through the area. Brigham Young then recalled his militia members from all corners of the Utah territory. Colonel Leiper returned to meet the approaching army and calmed the officers and solders who had been harassed by the Mormon militia. The arriving contingent of military observed no evidence of a Mormon war as they entered from the east, and the troops became very congenial toward the Latter-day Saints. The military contingent proceeded to move further down the road from Salt Lake City and set up Camp Floyd (to be known also as Frog Town) at Fairfield, which was located some forty-five miles southwest of the city.

The rebellion story was later learned to have been false. The story was prompted when Territorial Governor Brigham Young was said to have fallen into political conflict with a specific federal Judge, William W. Drummond. The judge became prompted to advise the U.S. president that the Latter Day Saints had launched a rebellion against the United States and it needed to be suppressed. The judge was later investigated and found to have falsely created a rebellion story to draw attention away from his own deceitfulness and extramarital love affair. When the true story became known, the attitudes changed among the military command and among settlers in the territory.

MASONRY IS RESURRECTED ...
UTAH GRAND LODGE CREATED

Some of the arriving soldiers at Camp Floyd were Master Masons. In 1859 they built themselves a crude 60 by 30 foot adobe building and called it Rocky Mountain Lodge 205 under a Missouri register. When the formation of a lodge was announced, 162 candidates were soon initiated. Lodge members not only practiced their Masonic craft, but they were also known for providing benevolence to help destitute emigrants as they passed through the area. It is interesting to note that Camp Floyd changed its name to Fort Crittenden right after Secretary of War John B. Floyd joined the Confederacy. Masonic activity seemed to die down with the news of the impending Civil War back east. This led to a new uncertainty to permeate across the Nation.

The Rocky Mountain Lodge No. 205 disbanded and sold all their paraphernalia to local Utahans. The Civil War did start a year later in 1861 and all territorial troops were recalled back east to participate. In 1862 a small garrison of federal troops again arrived in the area to establish Camp Douglas three miles east of Salt Lake City. The military presence in the area was established to insure that allegiance among the settlers stayed with the Union Cause during the Civil War.

In November 1865, James M. Ellis and fourteen Masons met in Salt Lake City and petitioned the Grand Lodge of Nevada (established in January 1865) in Virginia City to create a temporary Utah lodge by dispensation. Nevada Worshipful Grand Master, Joseph DeBell, responded affirmative in January 1866 but with a stipulation that "No Mormon be accepted for the degrees," and he later added, "or be admitted as a visitor." The stipulations were ordered due to an uncomfortable experience with Mormons living in and around Genoa[8], Nevada, formerly

---

[8] Mormon Station was established as a temporary trading post in the south west corner of the State of Deseret in 1850 by members of the Mormon Battalion: Abner Blackburn and Hampton Beatie. (Deseret was the territory expected to be claimed as a new Mormon state.) The outpost sat right on the California gold rush trail to Sutter's Mill where gold was discovered in 1848. John Reese and nephew Stephen Kinsey transported goods from Salt Lake City to Mormon Station and built a permanent trading post in 1851. Mormons settled in the area. A squatter's government was formed in 1854 and Brigham Young appointed Mormon Apostle Orson Hyde leader for the area. Orson Hyde changed the name to Genoa. Brigham Young recalled all Mormons back to Salt Lake City in 1857 when the potential of war with the U.S. Government was evident. Worshipful Grand Master LeBelle was recalling the 1857 incident when Nauvoo Militia unreasonably massacred 120 in the Fancher party in Mountain Meadows.

known as "Mormon Station." The Utahan Masons did meet and reluctantly endured this dispensation handicap. They endured the imposed restrictions until the Salt Lake Masons finally abandoned the Nevada Grand Lodge dispensation in September 1867.

Another Salt Lake City group of Masons, led by two Montana law partners, petitioned the Grand Lodge of Montana for a dispensation to open King Solomon Lodge in Salt Lake City. A dispensation was granted in October 1866, but the Montana Grand Lodge felt that because illegal polygamy existed in Utah, the name of King Solomon, who was a polygamist, was inappropriate. The Lodge was then chartered as Wasatch Lodge No. 8 named after the Wasatch Mountains outside of Salt Lake City. Unlike the Nevada dispensation, this Montana dispensation did not restrict Mormons from membership. Masons of the abandoned Nevada lodge remained determined to meet and practice their Masonic craft so they searched for a new dispensation source. An application was made to the Kansas Grand Lodge who did grant a dispensation on October 21, 1868 and Mt. Moriah Lodge No. 70 was born. After granting this dispensation however, the Kansas Grand Lodge was criticized nationwide by Masons for opening the door to Masonic "rogues," but the bitterness soon subsided.

In 1871, both the Wasatch Lodge and Mt Moriah Lodge worked together and requested a Colorado Grand Lodge dispensation to open a third Masonic lodge in the Utah Territory, which made way to establish the Grand of Utah. This dispensation was granted and Argenta Lodge No. 21 was established under a Colorado registry. The three established lodges then called for a convention in January 1872 in which the Territorial Grand Lodge of Utah was established. Wasatch Lodge became Lodge No. 1, Mt. Moriah Lodge became Lodge No. 2 and Argenta Lodge became Lodge No.

3 all under the new Utah registry. The Grand Lodge of Utah was actually formed by vigorous anti-Mormon Masons. These anti-Mormon Masons expressed disdain for the barbaric practice of polygamy. They also abhorred the invasive use of Masonic symbols on Mormon buildings—especially the beehive symbol. The beehive symbol was used by both Masons and Mormons to represent industry among all people. Brigham Young was especially inspired by the symbolic beehive because it represented true Industry and he established the beehive as a universal Mormon symbol. This symbol was placed everywhere throughout the city. The Masons took a serious stand soon after the Grand Lodge was organized when they issued their determination that the Latter-day Saints Church Temple Ceremony had actually been stolen from Freemasonry.

History then began to repeat in the new territory whereas non-Mormon settlers living in and around Salt Lake City started discriminating against the Latter-day Saints. It was beginning to sound much like it could be the beginning of another Mormon war. The ill feelings among the anti-Mormons grew from trying to tolerate the strict control imposed on all its members by the Latter-day Saints Church and the existence of the barbaric practice of open polygamy. The practice of polygamy was a crime at that time everywhere in the United States.

Polygamy became a violation of US law with the passing of the Morrill Anti Bigamy Act in 1862. However, the policing of this Act was difficult to enforce and resulted in Mormons deviating from the rule, so polygamy continued. To stem the tide of polygamy, Vermont Senator George Edmunds introduced a new bill to make all bigamist and polygamist felons. The bill became law in 1882 as the Edmunds Act. Over 1300 men were arrested following the passage of this bill and all were incarcerated for practicing polygamy. Polygamy then came to an official end.

The Mormon Church leaders worked desperately to make their Utah Territory, known to them as Deseret, an official State in the Union. As they repeatedly applied to the federal government for statehood, they were consistently turned down because they were illegally practicing polygamy in their designated territory. The LDS Church staunchly maintained that they had every right to live by their own fundamental biblical practice under the protection of the freedom of religion clause in the Bill of Rights. In 1887, the Edmunds-Tucker Bill was passed, which legally abolished many more practices used by the LDS Church including the Nauvoo Legion militia, and a legal mechanism was instigated to acquire church property previously disincorporated under the Morrell Act. The ultimate resistance for polygamy reached intensity to an extent that the Government was ready to step in and disenfranchise the Church and confiscate all its property. In October 1890, LDS Church President, Wilford Woodruff, issued the formal edict forbidding the practice of polygamy anywhere in the Church within the United States. When the polygamy edict became mandated and functioning throughout the church, Utah statehood was finally granted in 1896. But, hard-core Masons did not abandon their unofficial ban on allowing Mormons entry into Utah lodges or allow any Mason to remain a member of the Craft if they joined the Mormon Church.

Beginning with the first application for statehood in 1849, the Mormons applied to the Federal Government for a state land size mass actually larger than the present State of Utah and to name their state: "Deseret," a derivation of the word honeybee. The intent was to claim this territory or state land as Mormon land. They put together a very quick constitution to submit with their 1849 statehood application.

The assembled constitution was based on the State of Iowa constitution where the Mormons had temporarily lived. The submitted constitution was accepted. The Federal Government decided that the total land territory applied for was too ambitious and reduced its land size. The final government approval presented a smaller boundary for the state (the size we recognize today) and selected the name of Utah respectfully for the Ute Indians who were prominent in that area. Statehood was finally granted in 1896.

The first transcontinental railroad reached and traveled through Salt Lake City beginning in 1869 after the golden spike was placed at Promontory Point. This officially united the east with the west United States. The railroad then kept an incoming stream of additional new settlers to the region. Soon after the railroad arrived, the first Masonic Lodge building was constructed on South Main Street in Salt Lake City. After the lodge building was finished, other Masonic affiliations began to organize and move into the new building. One major new tenant was the Grand Encampment of Knights Templar (York Rite Orders that include: Royal Arch, Cryptic, Chivalric Mason degrees), which became chartered as Utah Chapter No. 1 in 1874. The Orient of Utah for the Ancient Accepted Scottish Rite for the Southern Masonic Jurisdiction (presenting the 4° through the 32°) later organized and became chartered in 1903. Over succeeding years Masonic membership had a slow but steady growth and more Masonic affiliates were added as tenants in the South Street Masonic Temple.

A little known contribution made by the Masons to Salt Lake City occurred in and around 1888 when the Grand Lodge of Masons established the Pioneer Library inside their building. This library was available to all who lived in Salt Lake City. Shortly after the library was established, the Ladies Literary Society of Salt Lake City succeeded in getting a bill passed in the territorial legislature in 1898 to set a tax levy that would support public libraries. The society, made up mostly of Mason's wives, purchased the Pioneer Library's 9,981 volume inventory for a very minimal sum and started the Salt Lake City Public Library System.

El Kalah Shrine, Ancient Arabic Order of the Nobles of the Mystic Shrine for North America, was chartered in 1891. The Shrine was established through the combined efforts of the York Rite Knights Templar Masons and a collection of Scottish Rite members living in and around Salt Lake City at that time. In those days a Mason had to be a member of either the Knights Templar or Scottish Rite to gain membership to the Shrine. Many of the originating Shriners were Utah Knights Templar and Scottish Rite Masons who had formally become Shrine members in adjoining States. In 1921, during the Imperial Session of the Shrine for North America, a nation-wide Shrine edict was accepted and approved to build and operate what was to become 22 non-profit Shrine Children's Orthopedic and Burns Hospitals across the United States. The Intermountain Unit of the Shrine Orthopedic Children's Hospital was finished and dedicated in Salt Lake City on January 25, 1925. The universal Shrine Children's Hospital's policy was conceived to accept any and all children needing medical orthopedic care regardless of their ability to pay for their medical care. The burn hospital accepts severely burned young and older individuals who need advanced and special burn care.

The Latter-day Saints opened their first hospital, the LDS Hospital in 1905 to serve local and surrounding area residents. As time progressed, a number of outstanding hospitals were also established in Salt Lake City including the well known Huntsman Cancer Clinic.

Masonic membership and affiliations steadily grew until they overflowed the South Main Street Masonic Temple. The lodges and Masonic affiliate organizations realized they needed a new building with more space. Planning for a larger new temple began in 1920. Temple board members carefully studied various building designs and determined that the new Temple should be a fresh design and not just a copy of other great temples. Plans were completed in1925 along with a land purchase at a location on South Temple Street. A very large and elegant Masonic Temple was built for $250,000 and dedicated in 1927 as Salt Lake City's finest example of Egyptian Revival Architecture. The building became the Masonic headquarters for the Utah Grand Lodge. The new Masonic Temple was located one mile west of the Salt Lake City Latter-day Saints Temple. This new Masonic Temple turned out to have a "building footprint" about the same relative size as the Grand Latter-day Saint's Temple.

In 1925, an uninviting "shadow" descended over Utah Masonry. The Utah Grand Lodge of Masons mandated an operating code for all in-state lodges stipulating that no Mormon would be permitted to enter or participate in Freemasonry at any time within the State of Utah. In response to the mandate the Latter-day Saint Church placed a ban preventing any Mason from joining the Latter Day Saints Church unless he gave up his Masonic allegiance. These restrictive bans applied only to men within the State of Utah. During the Utah ban, Mormons were fully permitted to participate in Freemasonry throughout all other states. This edict by the Latter-day Saints Church had been prompted by false characterizations displayed in national magazines, which reported and wrote that the LDS Church was operating too relevant to the Masonic Order. LDS church leaders stood by their principles of decorum and propriety from 1925 on and kept this operating code firmly in place. On the Masonic side, attempts were made to repeal the Grand Lodge resolution in 1927 but this repeal was rejected. This code remained in place in the LDS Church until 1984 when it was fully rescinded by the LDS leadership after studies were completed into the relationship between Mormon and Masons. Likewise, the Grand Lodge of Utah officially rescinded their ban in 1984.

Since those stressful days were written into the history books for the Utah Masons and the LDS, a new association and respect evolved between Mormons and Masons. Time seemed to create healing. In year 2007, Brother Glen Cook, a recognized Salt Lake City criminal defense attorney and Brigham Young University law school graduate, became the first member of The Church of Jesus Christ of Latter-day Saints to be elected as Utah Worshipful Grand Master of Masons. Most Worshipful Grand Master Cook became the 137th Worshipful Grand Master of Freemasonry in Utah.

CHARITY BEGINS AT HOME

As history advances and a new future begins . . . . The Latter-day Saints and Freemasonry, each in their own way, will keep supplying their benevolence, strength and service to all mankind.

Though I speak with the tongues of men and of angels and have not charity, I am become as sounding brass, or a tinkling cymbal.
And though I have the gift of prophecy, and understand all mysteries, and all knowledge; and though I have all faith, so that I could remove mountains, and have not charity, I am nothing.
And though I bestow all my goods to feed the poor, and though I give my body to be burned, and have not charity, it profit me nothing.
And now abideth faith, hope, charity, these three;
but the greatest of these is charity.

I Corinthians 13:1-3, 13

As Apostle Paul's directive was presented to the people of Corinth, his message also provides a present day directive for both Freemasonry and Latter-day Saints. There are places within the Masonic ritual where the above words can be found and these words underwrite the importance of charity in the life of Freemasons every day of their existence. Latter-day Saints have also abided by the Apostle's directive to build an outpouring of charity when and where it can be applied to their church family and to world wide needs in service to their Lord. Freemasonry has not only existed as a character building organization, but from its beginning it has been charitable in both brotherly love and benevolent help to mankind.

Freemasonry has a worldwide membership of 4,344,346 Masons by the latest count. 3,369,006 of those members reside within the United States and Canada, and this total also includes 1,852,503 Prince Hall (Black) Masons. A Mason's first obligation for charity is to come to the aid of a fellow Mason and his family, and especially to a deceased member's widow and orphans. Beyond brotherly love, a Mason reaches out to the needy across the world, and this includes their response to natural disasters to include destructive fires, floods, earthquakes and tornados. One memorable disaster was the Chicago fire in 1871 where some 300 people were killed, about 90,000 were left homeless and some $200 million in property was lost. Masons rose to the need and replaced lost lodge quarters and provided needed support to members as well as countless other people suffering losses.

Masonic philanthropy has steadily grown since 1727 when Masonry first arrived in the United States. Benevolent giving grew from a very simply giving of a stack of wood for heat and cooking to a needy widow, to erecting and manning large hospitals such as the Shriner Children's Orthopedic

Hospitals, Shriner Burn Treatment Hospitals and Scottish Rite Hospitals for Children. The total charity giving by Masons has always been made "out-of-pocket." Each day $1,400,000 has been expended in Masonic benevolence world wide. This totals some $511 million each year. These benevolent funds begin with the simple out-of-pocket donation given by member Masons. Beyond pocket donations, Masons freely volunteer time to work in money making projects such as the Shrine Circus or do special Masonic fund promotions. Masons are also busy working with Masonic related youth organizations to include: DeMolay for boys; Job's Daughters for girls; and Rainbow Girls. Some lodges can be found sponsoring youth baseball teams and academic bowl competitions. Aside from cash benevolences, Masons who are able, physically respond to tornados, floods, fires and attend to home repairs for the needy. Masons pay annual dues where normally over half the collected dues go to Masonic benevolence. There are some grateful members who benevolently leave land and property to be used for the good will and investment in Masonry. Lodge halls and meeting places are built, maintained and operated through the normal member dues. Beyond the very basic operating expenses, each Mason's time and talent is fully donated for the benevolent cause they are happy to fulfill. All hospitals and world wide clinics are provided totally free to the recipients. Doctors called to serve in the many hospitals are among the top in their specialty.

Mormon Charity also began when church members went to the aid of brother, sister or their family during their early stressful and beginning years. Through their history, there were many severe needs arising from time to time where help and sharing was needed. Early colonies were dependant on one another and mostly pooled physical help to build homes and their community. Shop owners were considerate of the community need by offering goods and services at an exchange that the fellow colony members could afford. Crops were shared whenever possible. During the exasperating local wars in Missouri and Illinois, both the church and Mormon families lost all their property and needed to depend on help from their neighbors to survive. Later the Mormons endured many hardships on their migration west when they had to depend on their brothers and sisters just to stay on the trail. When arriving in Salt Lake City, all Mormons were totally dependant on help from fellow Mormons. The physical outreach each Mormon learned and experienced now lives on today where church members donate their time to local charitable needs.

After the Latter-day Saints had built and settled in Salt Lake City, their church was seized in 1887 by the U.S. Government and all church assets and donations were confiscated. By 1907 the $2.3 million loss from the government seizure had been recovered by the faithful giving and generosity of the church members. The church began to prosper through responsible member tithing (10% of their income). From frugal beginnings good things by the Grace of the Lord began to happen. During the growth years in the 20th Century, the church began building Latter-day Saints temples in various locations around the country. The church invested some of their income in property holdings hoping that the investments would be profitable and would quickly increase their financial resources. They also began investing in farms and ranches where they would raise food to share with the world. As of late, the Latter-day Saints have one of the largest combined ranch and farm holdings in the nation.

The Latter-day Saints Church is very protective as to how their money is spent and invested. Some latest records show that there are 14,782,473 church members world wide with 6,321,416 members in the United States. The world wide annual income is estimated at $7 billion with $6.5

billion coming from the combined United States and Canada membership. The temple headquarters must maintain an asset sum of $35 billion to build and maintain their temples and meeting houses located world wide. However, with this income and asset picture, the Latter-day Saints do an extreme amount of benevolent help all around the world using both finances and member volunteers. $19,877,728 is spent annually on humanitarian charity and no administrative charges are added to charity expenses. Most all of the charity work locally and in the world is accomplished by able bodied Latter-day Saints who donate their time and efforts to fulfilling a charity call. Then, too, each Latter-day Saint has a covenant to serve two years as a church missionary somewhere in the world and each missionary pays all of their own expenses throughout their mission call. Disaster relief volunteers depart from their homes, work the disaster recovery, and return home all at their own personal expense. Some recent disasters responded to include the tsunami and earthquakes in Japan, typhoons in the Philippines; tornado in Southern United States; floods in Southern and Eastern United States. Mormon volunteers feel especially proud of the fact that they arrive at the disaster scene usually in advance of any other helping agency.

The interesting fact that brings Masons and Latter-day Saints together in benevolent support is the fact that some Latter-day Saints are Masons who contribute with generosity to Masonic benevolence. Some Masons are Latter-day Saints who tithe and give to their church causes. From this we can say that both organizations generously reach out to all mankind.

SYMBOLS—THE SIMILARATIES ARE INTERESTING

It is a fact that graphic symbols have existed since the beginning of time. Had it not been for symbols that survived time, archeologists and investigating researchers would not have been able to identify and learn about early civilizations. A symbol is defined as a visible sign by which a spiritual feeling, emotion, or idea impresses the viewer. Early Christians applied symbols to all their rites, ceremonies, and outward forms that bore religious meaning. In earlier history, Egyptians communicated their philosophic knowledge using mystic symbols. As Masonry developed, symbols allegorically were used to express a precept with a moral concept or attribute. In Masonic Lodges, for example, the plumb is a symbol of rectitude of conduct; the level to equality; the square to the square of virtue, the beehive to industry.

A symbol is designed so that it can be understood by any infant mind or simply an unknowledgeable mind. The touch and feel of the crafted image then expresses intended philosophy of the creator or organization. It is much like a sign does for a business. When organization symbols are publically presented, they represent the organization's internal meanings where each symbol is a kind of sacred language and displays instant organization recognition.

Freemasonry communicates mysteries by unique symbols:

Masonic symbols are generally only seen and observed within the Masonic lodge room and some only during the initiation ritual. The square and compass symbol or emblem is found proudly displayed outside and on the front of a Masonic lodge hall and on the lodge's signage. The square and compass is also found on jewelry rings and lapel pins worn by the Masonic Brotherhood, but symbols shown below will be seen only discretely outside of the Lodge Hall.

Of special note, there are particular locations and times when even the Masonic square and compass symbol has not been worn as a lapel pin, or engraved on a ring or displayed at the lodge hall exterior. For example, Freemasonry was condemned by Hitler in Germany beginning in 1926 at which time worthy and faithful Masons had to meet "underground" in complete secrecy. This also was true for operating Masonic lodges located in Japanese occupied countries during WWII. Masonic membership was prohibited in the Country of Belgium regardless of war conditions because

Belgium was Catholic dominated where Belgium currently uses the Catholic Canon Law of 1783 that denounced Masonry. This Belgium stature was a carry-over from a time when early Catholic Popes rejected Masons when they failed, as Templers [9], to contribute to building the Vatican. This canon law was changed by the Catholics in 1983 to again accept Masons. Belgium Masons continue to meet in secret. The forget-me-not flower lapel pin worn during WWII became the recognized symbol among all Masons and replaces wearing the square and compass in hostile areas in the world.

SQUARE & COMPASS: These two craft instruments are shown together as a moral teaching to square our actions and keep them within due bounds of the compass. Most always displayed together, they are the universally recognized and proper badge of a Master Mason.

The Square and Compass—the Symbol of Freemasonry—has been recognized and accepted as the Masonic emblem from the beginning of the 18th Century. The United States Patent Office took note of this in 1873. It told a flour manufacturer, and the world; "This device, so commonly worn and employed by Masons, has an established mystic significance, is universally recognized as existing, whether comprehended by all or not, it is not material to this issue. In view of the magnitude of the Masonic organization, it is impossible to divest its symbols, or at least this particular symbol—perhaps the best known of all—of its ordinary significance, wherever displayed." The manufacturer was denied the use of the Square and Compass as a trade-mark. The Square and

Compass are free to be used for any and all Masonic purposes.

THE SYMBOL "G": The letter "G" represents

Geometry. It is the science by which all labors are calculated and formed. To Masons it means the determination, definition, and proof of the order, it also represents the **G**rand Architect of the universe . . . God! The letter "G" was adopted to the order on the American continent in 1776.

THE SUN: The sun rules the day from sunup, through meridian day and to the sunset. As the sun rules the day, the Worshipful Master of the lodge governs the lodge. The sun is a symbol of sovereignty and absolute authority. The sunlight also represents the light and knowledge to each initiate.

The moon governs and rules the night in the universe. The Masonic Lodge represents the universe and the moon is the king of the starry hosts of the night. The moon, as well as sun are presided over by the Grand Architect of the Universe. The moon symbol has also been used by other ancient religions dating back to the Egyptians.

The Grip: It is a symbol of how Brother Masons can recognize each other at any time. The grip is unique and known only among Master Masons.

The Beehive: The beehive is an adopted symbol of industry to Master Masons. The busy hive represents the bee, the Master Mason works to receive wages to better support himself and his family, and to contribute to the relief of worthy distressed brethren, his widow and orphans. Among Egyptians it was the symbol of an obedient people and the bee alone had a king. The king ruled over the labor of the hive.

Pentalpha (of Pythagoras): This symbol is of the triple triangle. The letter "A" appears in five different positions. The Pythagoras doctrine was that all things occur by numbers as the number five appears in the pentalpha. As a Masonic symbol, the five pointed star indicates the bond of brotherly love that unites the entire fraternity This symbol is used by every Royal Arch Chapter and Eastern Star Chapter for its identity.

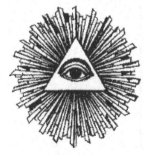

The All-Seeing Eye: This is an important symbol of the omni—present Deity. Freemasonry, along with the Hebrews and Egyptians use the "All-Seeing" eye to represent the eye of their deity: Eye To the Egyptian it symbolized The Eye of Osiris . . . . To the Hebrew it symbolizes the Eye of the Lord . . . . To the Freemasons it symbolizes the Eye of the Grand Architect of the Universe. The all-seeing eye first appeared in Masonry in 1797 when Thomas Smith Webb published it in the Freemason's Monitor. It represents the all seeing eye of God and is a reminder that a Mason's thoughts and deeds are always observed by The Grand Architect of the Universe. The eye in Masonry is normally shown inside a triangle.

[9] The original Knights Templar was formed in 1099 AD to serve as an Army in service for the Catholic Pope. This became the first organized army since the fall of the Roman Empire. By the combined efforts of King Phillip of France and Pope Clemet V, in 1307, Templar knights were arrested and incarcerated and then the lead knights were put on trial by inquisition. The inquisition resulted in convictions and the leaders were burned at the stake in Paris. The reason behind the arrests and inquisition was due to the Templar leaders not relinquishing their accumulated treasure hoard so that the king could build his Vatican. The Knights Templar wealth had been preserved just for Templar widow and orphan charity. Today, a new Vatican paper is expected to exonerate the Templar from the historical charges. Even though Templar descendants survived, Masons assumed and carried on the Knight's Templar regimen as one of their major Masonic Orders.

MORMON SYMBOLOGY

Researchers have studied the Mormon religion from its beginning and have not found but few specific explanations to the various symbols presented on the walls and in the ornaments of the Mormon Temples.

SQUARE AND COMPASS USE: The angel, Moroni, is represented as the weathervane on the original Nauvoo Temple steeple. A square and compass is mounted on the rod just above the angel. This is interpreted as a Masonic influence. This weathervane style was not repeated on the Salt Lake City Temple steeple nor on the 2001 reconstructed Nauvoo Temple. (Graphic, Sandra Tanner as presented from the Salt Lake Tribune, May 4, 2002, p C3)

TEMPLE SYMBOLS: The outside east wall of the Nauvoo Temple shows the full replication of symbols used on the early temple that was destroyed by wind and fire. The inverted pentagram can be viewed near the roof line. The sun stones

East Exterior Wall of the
new Nauvoo Temple

adorn the decretive columns. One sun stone survived the original temple fire and was located in a small park at the original temple site.

PENTAGRAM OR INVERTED STAR: The inverted stars on the New Nauvoo Temple exterior also adorn the exterior and interior of the Salt Lake City Temple. Not only are the stars adorning exterior walls, but the stars appear in upper windows and adorn the internal temple draperies. The pentagrams are thought to be emblems observed during Prophet Smith's early visions. As a related note, in 1855 a defrocked Catholic Priest in France re-identified the pentagram with the occult and Satanism. However, Profit Smith died a decade earlier and the new pentagram identity had no connection with Mormonism. Another interesting note from the reconstruction of the Nauvoo Temple, the window maker was confronted with the question whether or not to turn the stars upright and avoid the satanic inference. After due consideration, LDS President Hinckley directed that the stars would be placed inverted as intended in the original temple design.

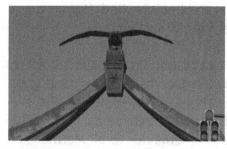

This is a view of the gate to Temple Square in Salt Lake City. It displays an eagle landing on a bee hive atop a keystone, which displays an inverted star or pentagram. The beehive and the inverted star are special symbols used by the LDS Church.

BEEHIVE: The beehive is found displayed throughout the LDS Temple in Utah. Brigham Young's family had revered the beehive in their earlier years when dealing with the occult. The beehive was a symbol of industry, and industry was an accepted virtue to mankind. Joseph Smith originally adopted the beehive as an accepted symbol for the LDS Church. Brigham Young added the beehive to the roof of his Salt Lake City home and it was also added to his personal seal. Brigham Young also connected the beehive with the land of "Deseret." When Brigham Young became governor of the Utah Territory, he petitioned Washington DC to have the new state named Deseret, but the government opted to name the new state after the Ute Indians (meaning: "people of the mountains"). The beehive became the Utah State symbol and the state became known as the "Beehive State."

THE ALL-SEEING EYE: The eye of Horus is the powerful symbol of wisdom, health and prosperity. Horas is represented as an Egyptian sun-god in the form of a falcon.

His right eye was the sun and his left eye was the moon. As a result of an injury and healing recovery of the left eye it becomes representative of the changing moon phases. Within the decorative arch above some Salt Lake LDS Temple entry doors you will find an "all-seeing eye" looking out from a burst of light. The eye also appears at other places in Salt Lake City on Mormon architecture. Both Mormons and Freemasons use the all-seeing-eye symbol.

THE GRIP: The hand grip to a Mormon is that symbol which binds them to their Endowment oaths. Various hand grips elude to the Aaronic priesthood, the penalty of life, the Melchiszedek priesthood and the Patriarchal Grip. The clasped hands shall serve as a reminder to all Mormons of their oath to the LDS Church. The hand grip is displayed in the decretive arch above some of the Salt Lake LDS Temple entry doors. The hand grip can also be observed displayed on other city buildings. The hand grip matches the hand grip symbol used and displayed by Freemasons.

THE SUN SYMBOL: The sunstone shown here adorned the original Nauvoo temple and survived the eventual temple demolition. It can be found on display in Nauvoo today. The new reconstructed Nauvoo temple  incorporated the sunstones at the head of the capitals as directed by Profit Smith's original design. Respective of the sun's face, Profit Smith was asked if the face looked like the face he saw in his vision? He replied: "Very near it!" Trumpet stones appear just above the sun and some call the trumpets cornucopias. Each sun had 40 points which was often used to represent a long period of time. The sunstones primarily refer to the vision of John in the Biblical Book of *Revelation*.

BIBLIOGRAPHY

MASONIC RECOURCES:

Holmes, Noel. *"The Morgan Affair,"* Maryland: The Short Talk Bulletin—Vol. XI, Masonic Service Association, March, 1933 No.3 (internet)' Grand Lodge of British Columbia and Yukon.

Brown, Matthew B., *"Exploring the Connection Between Mormons and Masons,"* Covenant Communications, 2009.

Kelly, Bruce. *"The Age of Enlightenment,"* brucekelly. com, (internet): 2012; (search) Enlightenment or Age of Enlightenment

Keene, Michael, *"The Strange Connection between William Morgan (An Anti-Mason) And Joseph Smith (A Mormon),"* EnzineArticles.com, 2012, http://EzineArticles.com/?expert=Michael_Keene

Litersky, Nicholas S.; "Freemasonry and Mormons;" (internet) signaturebookslibrary.org/?=418

Mackey, Albert G., MD, *"Encyclopedia of Freemasonry and Its Kindred Sciences"* Philadelphia: McClure Publishing, 1927

Masonic World, "Masonic Relief, Charity and You," (internet) www.masonicworld.com/education/articles/masonic_relief.htm

Masons of California, *"Freemasonry in Utah"* (Masonic History), 2011-2012 speculativemasonry.org/category/Masonic-history/

Moore, Carrie A., *"A Mormon Mason: New grand master is the first in a century who is LDS,"* Salt Lake City: Deseret News, 2008 (Internet source)

Morgan, Capt. William, *"Illustrations of Masonry,"* Internet available @: www.utlm.org/onlinebooks/captmorgansfreemasonrycontents.htm

Morris, S. Brent, "Masonic Philanthropies, A tradition of Caring, Second Edition," The Supreme Councils, 33°, N.M.J. & S.M.J., 1997

Multiple Authors, *"Captain Morgan and the Masonic Influence in Mormonsim,"* Chapter 13, (pages 151-169) from *The Mormon Kingdom Vol 1* (Internet: www.utlm.org/onlineresources/mormonkingdomvol1ch13masonicinfluence.htm)

Parisi, Attilio G., *"Freemasonry in Utah,"* et el, www.media.utah.edu/UHE/m/MASONRY,FREE.html

Thomas, Michael S.; "Freemasonry and Mormonism;" www.phoenixmasonry.org/freemasonry_and_mormonism

Wikipedia, "Enoch (ancestor of Noah)," (internet) July 2013

Wikipedia, "Mormonism and Freemasonry," (internet) April 2012

Wikipedia, "Salt Lake Masonic Temple," (internet) June 2013

Zufall, William R., *"The Morgan Affair/Anti-Masonic Excitement"*, available on the internet.

MORMONS:

Anderson, R.L., & Faulring, S.H, "The Profit Joseph Smith and His Plural Wives," FARMS Review—Vol. 10, Issue 2, pages 67-104: BYU Maxwell Institute, 1998

Dunn, Loren C, Elder of the Seventy, *"Symbolism: Symbols in architecture of the temple are a 'means of teaching.'* February 1993; Church News, The Church of Jesus Christ of Latter Day Saints. (Deseret News); www.ldschurchnews.com/articles/23605Symbolism

FAIRMormon, "Mormonism and temples/Symbols on the Nauvoo Temple",

En.fairmormon.org/Mormonism_and_temples/Symbols_on_the_Nauvoo-Temple, see Endnotes. August 2012

Groat, Joel B., "Occultic and Masonic Influence in Early Mormonism," 1996, Institute For Religious Research (Internet available)

In Plain Site: "Section 11 . . . Cults/Mormonism, "Mormon Symbols," (Internet source) www.inplainsite.org, April 2012.

LDS Social Network, "Quotes by Joseph Smith: 'Charity'," www.lds.net/forums/scripture-study-forums/33688-quotes-joseph

Leazer, Gary, "Mormon—Belief Bulletin," Atlanta: Home Mission Board, SBC: 1983, 1990

McLean, Kimberly, "Of Masons and Mormons: 'The Solomon Key' offers controversial sequel." Universe (universe.byu.edu), May 2006

Scharffs, Gilbert W., PhD, "Setting the Record Straight—Mormons & Masons," Orem, UT, Millennial Press, 2006

Signature Book's Library, "Freemasonry and Mormons," (Internet) 2013

Signature Book's Library, "Sidney Rigdon," (internet) 2013

Tanner, Sandra, "Masonic Symbols and the LDS Temple," (internet), (find under topic)

Utah History to Go; Embray, Jessie L.; "The History of Polygamy"; (internet)

Wikipedia, "Angel Moroni," (internet) June 2013

Wikipedia, "Church of Christ (Whitmerite);" (Internet)

Wikipedia, "Death of Joseph Smith,"

Wikipedia, "Finances of The Church of Jesus Christ of Latter-day Saints," (internet)

Wikipedia, "Genoa, Nevada," (internet)

Wikipedia, "George M. Hinkle;" (Internet)

Wikipedia, "Great Apostasy'"

Wikipedia, "Harmonica gun," (Internet)

Wikipedia, "History of the Latter Day Saint movement," April 2012 (internet)

Wikipedia, "Jonathon Browning;" (Internet)

Wikipedia, "Joseph Smith," /42: http://en.widipedia.org/wiki/Joseph_Smith, (internet) 2012

Wikipedia, "LDS Humanitarian Services," (internet)

Wikipedia, "Mormon Trail," (internet)

Wikipedia, "Mountain Meadows massacre," (internet)

Wikipedia, "Nauvoo Temple," (internet) June 2013

Wikipedia, "Oliver Cowdery" (internet) June 2013

Wikipedia, "Salt Lake Temple," (internet)

Wikipedia, "Sidney Rigdon," (internet) June 2013

Wikipedia, "State of Deseret" (internet) July 2013

Wikipedia, "(Whitmerite) Church of Christ," (internet) June 2013

Wishnatsky, Martin, *"Mormonism—A Latter Day Deception,"* see: Apostle John A. Widtsoe, Utah Genealogical and Historical Magazine, April, 1921, <u>www.goodmorals.org/ mormons/index.asp?poetlist=chapterone.htm</u>.

Printed in the United States
by Bookmasters

Printed in the United States
By Bookmasters